the pursuit of style

advice & musings
from america's
top fashion designers

**THE COUNCIL OF FASHION
DESIGNERS OF AMERICA**

illustrations by bil donovan

ABRAMS, NEW YORK

love is life
Diane ♥

Life is a journey, and we are all part
of the landscape of fashion. Inspiration
comes from every facet of life: nature,
art, movies, books. . . . This book
will give you a moment of intimacy
with American fashion designers,
and I hope the answers will inspire you.

—DIANE VON FURSTENBERG, PRESIDENT OF THE CFDA

Though I'm inspired by all mediums of art, I have perhaps been the most inspired by my human connections. The most special of these relationships are the ones that I've made with our members at the CFDA. I began at the CFDA the same week as Diane von

Furstenberg, who serves as our president, and throughout the years, we've had the incredible opportunity to work side by side. She has been an amazing partner in our work on behalf of American fashion, but more importantly, she has been a great friend who I've learned so much from.

Running the CFDA can be daunting, but with her advice and wisdom, I always feel supported and energized. It's these feelings that I hope you, too, can take away from our members.

From fashion, style, and career advice to more personal advice on wisdom and love, this book is a compilation of the experiences that define who we are as humans. Though the work of designing is surely an integral part of all our members' lives, it's other arenas of life—such as love, early memories, and early career setbacks and successes—that have influenced their work. We urged them to dig deep and share musings and advice from these vast experiences.

We set out with the goal of learning more from our renowned group of American fashion designers, and we couldn't have imagined the responses generated. I've worked with so many of these designers throughout the years, and I was still surprised to learn about their experiences growing up or about things they have learned about themselves over the course of their lives. And though you might be most familiar with some designers through their clothing and accessories, this book will acquaint you in an up-close-and-personal way.

There are some designers who are new members—they may be young, but their advice is wise. And then there are fashion luminaries who have cultivated years of wisdom to share. Some answers are funny, others are sentimental. But one thing is for sure—they are all inspiring.

I hope that these experiences impart a bit of what our members have learned upon their journeys, but it is up to you to make your own lessons and your own journey. Each piece of advice not only inspired me but also made me feel alive. Go after what you believe in, so that, like the designers in this book, you can record what you're most grateful for, how you define success, what makes you afraid, and more importantly, what makes *you* feel alive.

—**STEVEN KOLB**, CHIEF EXECUTIVE OFFICER OF THE CFDA

Fashion uses a language that's a mystery to many, but we all understand how it helps us tell a story about ourselves that everyone can see. It's the foundation of something highly personal that we often refer to as *style*. Living with style transports the fantasy of fashion to the everyday hustle of life. From your

INTRODUCTION

office to your most intimate moments, wearing clothes that represent your spirit brings the designer into a conversation about the roles that we play every day: the feminine strength of Diane von Furstenberg; the minimalist chic of Narciso Rodriguez; the effortless urbanity of Donna Karan; the fierce elegance of

Eddie Borgo; the classic American attitude of Ralph Lauren, Tory Burch, and Jenna Lyons at J. Crew. When we put on the right clothing, it feels as if it has the power to reveal not only who we are but who we want to be.

For all that our clothes can say about us, we know so little about the inspirations and aspirations of the designers themselves. What drives them—their passions, taboos, icons, cultural fascinations, personal quirks, spiritual paths, and earthly obsessions—to dedicate their lives to making our lives look and feel fabulous? I've been fortunate enough to wear the exquisite results born from the hard work of so many amazing designers and am so lucky to call them friends and mentors, not just about fashion, but also about filling life with beauty and creativity in every aspect. Through touching personal stories and funny quips, this book shows the character and standards of style of some of the brightest stars in American fashion as they give their simple advice on what matters the most: passion, creativity, and being the best version of yourself you can possibly be.

—JESSICA ALBA

Reem Acra
Alexa Adams, OHNE TITEL
Waris Ahluwalia, HOUSE OF WARIS
Simon Alcantara
Joseph Altuzarra, ALTUZARRA
Carolina Amato,
  CAROLINA AMATO INC.
Mary Ann Restivo, MARY ANN
  RESTIVO LTD.
Greg Armas, ASSEMBLY NEW YORK
Brian Atwood
Lubov Azria, BCBG MAX AZRIA
Yigal Azrouel,
  YIGAL AZROUEL INC.
Jeffrey Banks
John Bartlett
Gaby Basora, TUCKER
Dennis Basso
Michael Bastian
Shane Baum, LEISURE SOCIETY
Bradley Bayou,
  BRADLEY BAYOU COUTURE
Erin Beatty, SUNO
Stacey Bendet,
  ALICE & OLIVIA BY STACEY BENDET

Alexandre Birman
Kenneth Bonavitacola
Eddie Borgo,
  EDDIE BORGO JEWELRY
Monica Botkier, BOTKIER
Barry Bricken,
  DAN-MAR MFG CO. INC
Sophie Buhai, VENA CAVA
Tory Burch
Stephen Burrows
Kevin Carrigan,
  CALVIN KLEIN INC.
Salvatore Cesarani
Amy Chan, AMY 8 CHAN
Natalie Chanin, ALABAMA CHANIN
Georgina Chapman, MARCHESA
Ron Chereskin
Dao-Yi Chow, PUBLIC SCHOOL
Martin Cooper, BELSTAFF
Maria Cornejo,
  ZERO BY MARIA CORNEJO
Francisco Costa,
  CALVIN KLEIN INC.
Jeffrey Costello,
  COSTELLO TAGLIAPIETRA

Erica Courtney,
  ERICA COURTNEY INC.
Steven Cox, DUCKIE BROWN
Keren Craig, MARCHESA
Louis Dell'Olio, LDO CO LTD
Rachel Dooley, GEMMA REDUX
Keanan Duffty
Stephen Dweck,
  STEPHEN DWECK JEWELRY
Luis Fernandez, @LUISFERN5
Erin Fetherston,
  FETHERSTON DESIGN GROUP
Cheryl Finnegan,
  VIRGINS SAINTS AND ANGELS
Jennifer Fisher
R. Scott French
Robert Geller
Tess Giberson
Flora Gill, OHNE TITEL
Adriano Goldschmied,
  CITIZENS OF HUMANITY
Nicholas Graham
Henry Grethel, HG DESIGN INT LLC
Ulrich Grimm, CALVIN KLEIN INC.
Prabal Gurung

Jeff Halmos, SHIPLEY + HALMOS
Douglas Hannant
Joan Helpern, JOAN & DAVID
Stan Herman
Carolina Herrera
Tommy Hilfiger,
    TOMMY HILFIGER GROUP
Carole Hochman
Mara Hoffman
Sang A Im-Propp
Henry Jacobson
Lisa Jenks
Betsey Johnson
Gemma Kahng
Norma Kamali
Jen Kao
Donna Karan
Shaun Kearney, SHAUN-M-
    KEARNEY CONSULTING
Rod Keenan, ROD KEENAN
    NEW YORK
Monica Rich Kosann
Reed Krakoff
Michel Kramer-Metraux,
    MICHEL CRAVAT
Devi Kroell, DAX GABLER
Blake Kuwahara,
    FOCUS GROUP WEST
Derek Lam
Adrienne Landau
Liz Lange
Ralph Lauren
Robert Lee Morris
Nanette Lepore
Michael Leva
Marcella Lindeberg
Johan Lindeberg, BLK DENIM
Deborah Lloyd,
    KATE SPADE NEW YORK
Pamela Love
Laurie Lynn Stark, CHROME HEARTS
Jenna Lyons, J. CREW
Catherine Malandrino
Isaac Manevitz, BEN-AMUN
Melissa Joy Manning,
    MELISSA JOY MANNING, INC.
Lisa Mayock, VENA CAVA,
    VIVA VENA
Mary McFadden
David Meister
Jonathan Meizler,
    TITLE OF WORK

Gilles Mendel, J. MENDEL
Jennifer Meyer
Stefan Miljanic, GILDED AGE
Nicole Miller
Rebecca Minkoff
Lauren Moffatt
Bibhu Mohapatra
Laura Mulleavy, RODARTE
Josie Natori
Irene Neuwirth,
    IRENE NEUWIRTH JEWELRY
David Neville, RAG & BONE
Roland Nivelais
Vanessa Noel
Maggie Norris,
    MAGGIE NORRIS COUTURE
Michelle Ochs
Maxwell Osborne,
    PUBLIC SCHOOL
Max Osterweis, SUNO
Shimon Ovadia
Ariel Ovadia, OVADIA & SONS
John Patrick,
    ORGANIC BY JOHN PATRIK
Monique Péan
Gabriela Perezutti, CANDELA
Patty Perreira, BARTON PERREIRA
Lisa Perry
Mary Ping
Zac Posen,
    ZAC POSEN, HOUSE OF Z LLC.
James Purcell
Billy Reid
Monica Rich Kosann
Judith Ripka,
    JUDITH RIPKA JEWELRY
Eddie Rodriguez
Narciso Rodriguez
Robert Rodriguez
Pamella Roland
Charlotte Ronson
Lela Rose
Kara Ross, KARA ROSS NEW YORK
Ippolita Rostagno, IPPOLITA
Christian Roth, CHRISTIAN ROTH
    EYEWEAR FOR OPTICAL AFFAIRS
Cynthia Rowley
Rachel Roy
Ralph Rucci
Selima Salaun, SELIMA OPTIQUE
Lisa Salzer, LULU FROST
L'Wren Scott

Tadashi Shoji
Daniel Silver, DUCKIE BROWN
Tabitha Simmons
Christian Siriano
Michael Smaldone
Amy Smilovic, TIBI
Michelle Smith, MILLY
Jodie Snyder Morel, DANNIJO
Maria Snyder
Danielle Snyder, DANNIJO
Mimi So, MIMI SO INTERNATIONAL
Peter Som
Shelly Steffee
Scott Sternberg,
    BAND OF OUTSIDERS
Jill Stuart
Anna Sui
Koi Suwannagate
Daiki Suzuki, ENGINEERED
    GARMENTS/NEPENTHES
Albertus Swanepoel,
    ALBERTUS SWANEPOEL LLC
Robert Tagliapietra,
    COSTELLO TAGLIAPIETRA
Elie Tahari
Rebecca Taylor
Yeohlee Teng, YEOHLEE INC.
Olivier Theyskens, THEORY
Monika Tilley
Rafe Totengco, RAFE NEW YORK
Trina Turk
Kay Unger, KAY UNGER DESIGN
Cynthia Vincent
Diane von Furstenburg
Patricia von Musulin,
    PATRICIA VON MUSULIN SIGNUM
Marcus Wainwright,
    RAG & BONE
Vera Wang
Edward Wilkerson,
    LAFAYETTE 148 NEW YORK
Araks Yeramyan, ARAKS
Gerard Yosca,
    GERARD YOSCA JEWELRY
David Yurman
Rachel Zoe
Italo Zucchelli, CALVIN KLEIN INC.

PART 1

style

Opulent, creative, bohemian, artistic, bold
—ADRIENNE LANDAU

The ultimate achievement. You either have it or you don't.
—BRIAN ATWOOD

A mix of modern shapes with nostalgic influences
—RON CHERESKIN

Effortless and solid
—MARY PING

Understanding the rules and breaking them just enough to have a voice of your own
—MAX OSTERWEIS

Style that beats the test of time
—GABRIELA PEREZUTTI

Authentic and appropriate to its purpose.
—CAROLINA AMATO

Sophisticated, irreverent, and true to each woman's own
—JOSEPH ALTUZARRA

An individual thing— it is relative. True style is really about daring to be you.
—MARTIN COOPER

Personal, creative, and expressive, with a touch of drama
—KEREN CRAIG

TO ME, CLASSIC STYLE IS

Timeless and consistent
—EDDIE BORGO

Simple, effortless yet decidedly beautiful
—DEVI KROELL

Universal
—DONNA KARAN

The essence of style of a given period
—MONIKA TILLEY

Effortless
—MICHELLE OCHS

Greece, fifth century BC
—MARY McFADDEN

Being unapologetic about what you want to wear and how you want to wear it
—JEN KAO

When it looks effortless
—MONICA RICH KOSANN

All about taking an iconic piece and turning it on its head—combining my Parisian atelier background with my love for American sportswear
—MICHELLE SMITH

Keeping it simple and clean
—NARCISO RODRIGUEZ

Something beautiful
and balanced that is
culturally standardized
—OLIVIER THEYSKENS

Something that
never bores me
—PATRICIA VON MUSULIN

A white shirt, 501
Levis, great shoe,
perfect watch—
male or female
—RALPH RUCCI

A part of cultural
zeitgeist that has
managed to rise to the
top (and stay there)
for a consistent and
considerable amount of
time, owing its longevity
to its own versatility
and universal message
—STEFAN MILJANIC

The perfect balance
of fashion and history
—STAN HERMAN

You're asking
someone who wears
tutus to work! I would
say classic depends
on the individual.
—STACEY BENDET

A less-is-more
aesthetic
—PATTY PERREIRA

Navy, olive, and
white—a style that has
lasting worth, timeless
—DAIKI SUZUKI

timeless

Never trying too hard.
Classic style should never
look or seem forced.
—R. SCOTT FRENCH

Clean simple lines,
great tailoring, and
a flattering fit
—SIMON ALCANTARA

Staying true to your
personality. It is someone
that does not lose their
originality and individuality
by following trends.
—CAROLINA HERRERA

Putting something
that makes you happy
on and knowing that
you can wear it forever
and still love it and
look good
—STEPHEN DWECK

Wearing an outfit
you could have worn
twenty years ago, or
twenty years from now
—SOPHIE BUHAI

A god-given gift
—DAVID NEVILLE

Timeless. It's cool
today and it will be
cool in twenty years.
It's a worn pair of
jeans, a tweed blazer,
or an old hunting
jacket. Things that get
better with age.
—SHIMON OVADIA

Relevant to what we
each do and hope to
achieve in the world
—JOAN HELPERN

Eclectic, vibrant, iconic, unique, and global
—RAFE TOTENGCO

Minimal-meets-gothic-meets-vintage
—BLAKE KUWAHARA

Clean, relaxed, masculine, feminine, a bit minimal
—AMY SMILOVIC

Preppy with a modern twist
—TOMMY HILFIGER

Classic, whimsical, neat, off-kilter, and simple
—GERARD YOSCA

IN FIVE WORDS, MY PERSONAL STYLE

Relaxed urban cowboy
—DAVID YURMAN

Urban. Black. Modern. Flexible. Day into night.
—DONNA KARAN

Easy, comfortable, boyish, modern, sophisticated
—VERA WANG

Monocratic, tough, understated, simple minimalist
—MAXWELL OSBORNE

Repetitive, simple, comfortable, easy, tailored
—JEFF HALMOS

Feminine and a
little tomboyish

—CHARLOTTE RONSON

Colorful, textural, quirky,
sophisticated, and fun

—LELA ROSE

Classic, relaxed,
uniform,
quiet, simple

—DEREK LAM

Whoever
I want
to be
when I
wake up

—RALPH LAUREN

CAN BE DESCRIBED AS

"Minimal
gangster"

—MICHELLE OCHS

Eclectic, artistic,
habitual, yet
ever-changing
and instinctual

—PATTY PERREIRA

Clean, spare,
detailed, preppy,
effortless

—R. SCOTT FRENCH

Classic elegance
always perfectly accessorized

—MARY ANN RESTIVO

Uniform—it's
the same every day

—REED KRAKOFF

Classic elegant French LA second-hand

—SOPHIE BUHAI

Connoisseur with a visionary twist
—LUBOV AZRIA

Casually neat— very Virgo

—STAN HERMAN

Modern, minimal, happy, playful, and lots of color!

—LISA PERRY

Vibrant, graphic, uncom- plicated, West Coast

—TRINA TURK

Classic, bohemian, feminine, romantic, tailored
—JODIE SNYDER

Subtle, classic, grandfatherish, honest, refined

—SHANE BAUM

Chic but
somewhat dirty

—PATRICIA VON MUSULIN

Punk, sexy,
sparkly,
pretty, pure

—BETSEY JOHNSON

Tacky diamond jeans and a "kick-ass" "T"

—BETSEY JOHNSON

Pajamas

—CAROLE HOCHMAN

A wetsuit

—CYNTHIA ROWLEY

My navy blazer and a tie

—DENNIS BASSO

Sky-high heels

—ERICA COURTNEY

A bodysuit and skinny pants

—DONNA KARAN

Sneakers and baseball hat

—DAO-YI CHOW

I FEEL MOST MYSELF WHEN I'M WEARING

My own clothes

—DIANE VON FURSTENBERG

A perfectly worn-in pair of jeans with a crisp, white button-down, a navy blue blazer, and loafers

—TOMMY HILFIGER

My fedora

—EDDIE BORGO

Leggings, t-shirts, a beanie, and incredible outerwear

—VERA WANG

A dress and riding around town on my bike

—LELA ROSE

Slim-fit, washed jeans with a cashmere T-shirt

—EDDIE RODRIGUEZ

A floaty, ethereal dress in pale colors. I once did a series of pleated chiffon dresses and skirts in muted pastels like blush and sky gray; those are always my favorite go-to pieces. They feel lighter than air.
—ERIN FETHERSTON

I am designing
—FRANCISCO COSTA

My riding boots at the ranch
—GABRIELA PEREZUTTI

Riding my bicycle
—GABY BASORA

My glasses
—GERARD YOSCA

Feathers
—IPPOLITA ROSTAGNO

A T-shirt and trainers
—JOSEPH ALTUZARRA

Jewelry. And a lot of it.
—JUDITH RIPKA

501s, a men's T, and a big necklace
—RACHEL DOOLEY

Black cigarette pants, a unique black jacket, amazing costume jewelry, and the best white shirt
—KAY UNGER

Vivienne Westwood bondage pants
—KEANAN DUFFTY

Red lipstick
—KOI SUWANNAGATE

Heels
—L'WREN SCOTT

A big colorful dress—something with a lot of fabric that's a little dramatic, maybe even slightly ridiculous. Fashion should never be too serious.
—LISA MAYOCK

Something new and something old
—LUBOV AZRIA

Jodhpurs
—MAGGIE NORRIS

Jeans, a T-shirt, and boots
—MARA HOFFMAN

My stacking diamond slice rings
—MELISSA JOY MANNING

My signature anchor necklace
—NANETTE LEPORE

Polka dots
—NICK GRAHAM

Nothing
—OLIVIER THEYSKENS

A lot of jewelry
—PAMELA LOVE

A smile
—PATTY PERREIRA

A bathrobe
—RACHEL ROY

Silk tee, pants, stilettos, a great lip color, and red nails
—REBECCA TAYLOR

My Sebago Docksides and a pair of broken-in slim khaki pants
—R. SCOTT FRENCH

PJs
—SCOTT STERNBERG

A dress, fuchsia lipstick, sunglasses, and high heels

—SELIMA SALAUN

My sunglasses—can't leave the house without them regardless of the weather

—SHAUN KEARNEY

Black

—NICOLE MILLER

Espadrilles, high-waisted deadstock Levis, a French twist, a leotard, and a perfect nineties blazer

—SOPHIE BUHAI

A pair of great narrow loom, 13 oz. denim selvedge jeans

—STEFAN MILJANIC

My H&M black zip-hoodie

—STEPHEN BURROWS

Nothing

—WARIS AHLUWALIA

A tuxedo

—ZAC POSEN

A mash-up of
Patti Smith and
Slim Keith
—AMY SMILOVIC

Tilda Swinton
—LISA SALZER

James Dean
—RON CHERESKIN

Coco Chanel
—CAROLE HOCHMAN

Fred Astaire
—DAIKI SUZUKI

Sybil Yurman, my
wife. Always in
the back of my mind,
I ask, "Would
Sybil like it? Would
Sybil wear it?"
—DAVID YURMAN

A strong, confident
woman with an
independent point
of view
—TESS GIBERSON

Diana Vreeland
—DEBORAH LLOYD

Anyone with
character
—ITALO ZUCCHELLI

Carine Roitfeld
—JOSEPH ALTUZARRA

Georgia O'Keeffe
—LISA JENKS

Jac, my wife
—LOUIS DELL'OLIO

Patti Smith
—LAURA MULLEAVY

MY STYLE MUSE IS

Charlotte Rampling in
Night Porter, Loulou de
la Falaise, Jane Fonda
in *Klute,* Faye Dunaway
in *The Thomas Crown
Affair,* Romy Schneider
in *The Swimming Pool,*
Catherine Deneuve in
Belle de Jour
—CATHERINE MALANDRINO

I always thought
Anita Pallenberg had
the coolest rock style.
—ANNA SUI

Millicent Rogers
—CYNTHIA VINCENT

Iman—because of
her love of fashion
and her super style.
She represents chic,
modern, and elegant
with a twist.
—EDWARD WILKERSON

Camilla Nickerson
—FRANCISCO COSTA

Perry Ellis
—GERARD YOSCA

Diane von Furstenberg
—JENNIFER MEYER

Gregory Peck in
Roman Holiday
—MICHEL KRAMER-
METRAUX

Cleopatra or Marilyn
Monroe—but Marilyn
Monroe wins because
she is a reality whereas
Cleopatra's style is a
bit of a myth.
—OLIVIER THEYSKENS

It's always changing, but I love looking to both real and fictional women for inspiration. It could be anyone from Alice in Wonderland to Mia Farrow.

—ERIN FETHERSTON

A potent mix of
Audrey Hepburn,
Catherine
Deneuve, Ava
Gardner, and
Tilda Swinton
—PRABAL GURUNG

The
modern,
multi-
tasking,
multi-
committed
human
being
—JOAN HELPERN

Brigitte Bardot and Jane Birkin
—RACHEL ZOE

Debbie Harry
—REBECCA TAYLOR

Marlon Brando was pretty cool
—JOHAN LINDEBERG

Madonna
—ROBERT RODRIGUEZ

My wife, Dee
—TOMMY HILFIGER

Veruschka
—DANIELLE SNYDER

Cary Grant
—ROD KEENAN

Ali MacGraw
—STAN HERMAN

My mother—she has
impeccable style!
—TORY BURCH

Ernest Hemingway
—ADRIANO GOLDSHMIED

David Bowie
meets Porfirio
Rubirosa

—SIMON ALCANTARA

The everyday
woman

—TADASHI SHOJI

A confident woman

—DIANE VON FURSTENBERG

Catherine the Great
—ADRIENNE LANDAU

Marina Abramovic.
Her strength is
so pervasive in
both her work and
appearance.
—ALEXA ADAMS

Eleanor Roosevelt
—ARAKS YERAMYAN

Yoshitomo Mara
—DAIKI SUZUKI

William Faulkner
—BILLY REID

Talitha Getty
—CYNTHIA VINCENT

James Brown.
He slays me.
—JENNA LYONS

Tilda Swinton
—LISA SALZER

Ronald Reagan
—HENRY GRETHEL

Amelia Earhart
—LAUREN MOFFATT

Seventies-era
Anjelica Huston
—LISA MAYOCK

Jane Birkin
—LUBOV AZRIA

Frida Kahlo
—MARA HOFFMAN

Brigitte Bardot
—MARCELLA LINDEBERG

IF I COULD DRESS ONE PERSON, DEAD OR ALIVE, IT WOULD BE

Edie Sedgwick
—BRADLEY BAYOU

Jackie Kennedy
—CAROLE HOCHMAN

Marilyn Monroe
—KATE MULLEAVY

Cinderella
—CHERYL FINNEGAN

The Duchess of
Devonshire
—CAROLINA AMATO

Lucille Ball. She
makes us laugh
so hard we overlook
that she was
wearing beautiful
custom couture.
—JAMES PURCELL

Babe Paley.
She is emblematic
of timeless
elegance and style.
—KARA ROSS

T. E. Lawrence
—MARTIN COOPER

Isabella Rossellini
—MARY ANN RESTIVO

Greta Garbo
—MARY MCFADDEN

Cary Grant
—JEFFREY BANKS

Edie Sedgwick
—MICHAEL LEVA

Faye Dunaway
—MICHAEL SMALDONE

Michelle Obama,
Kate Middleton
—RACHEL ZOE

Elizabeth Taylor
—TABITHA SIMMONS

Joan of Arc or
Cleopatra
—SOPHIE BUHAI

Natalie Portman.
Not only is she
stunning, but she
is also intelligent,
talented, and
philanthropic.
—MONIQUE PÉAN

Stevie Nicks
—PAMELA LOVE

David Bowie
—REBECCA TAYLOR

Alive
—NICK GRAHAM

Françoise Hardy
—YIGAL AZROUËL

Virginia Woolf
—STAN HERMAN

Miles Davis.
I love his amazing
taste in eyewear.
—PATTY PERREIRA

Marie Antoinette
—ULRICH GRIMM

Elvis
—STEVEN COX

Cleopatra. She would
allow me to literally
drip her in my jewels
from head to toe.
—MIMI SO

Sophia Loren
—NANETTE LEPORE

Ava Gardner,
Rita Hayworth,
Dorothy Dandridge
—STEPHEN BURROWS

Edith Beale
—CHRISTIAN SIRIANO

Gwyneth Paltrow
—ROBERT LEE MORRIS

Steve McQueen . . .
of course
—SELIMA SALAUN

Kate Moss
—MONICA BOTKIER

Lucille Ball—
"I Loved Lucy"
—STEPHEN DWECK

Romy Schneider
—TORY BURCH

I don't think I could
choose one. Names
like Gertrude Stein,
Georgia O'Keeffe, Mary
Magdalene, Zora Neale
Hurston, Christiane
Amanpour, Alice
Waters, Mavis Staples,
Christina Hendricks,
Chelsea Clinton, and
her mother, Hillary
Clinton (without a
pantsuit) all come
to mind.
—NATALIE CHANIN

Shwe-shwe fabric
from South Africa

—ALBERTUS SWANEPOEL

Anything with structure

—AMY SMILOVIC

Raw materials like
metal and pewter

—ISAAC MANEVITZ

MY FAVORITE FABRIC TO WEAR / TO WORK WITH IS

Linen—means I'm
somewhere warm

—WARIS AHLUWALIA

Copper. It's industrial and
natural all at once.

—RACHEL DOOLEY

My favorite brushed zebra
alligator from France

—SANG A IM-PROPP

My favorite fabric to wear is a soft, lightweight linen on a hot summer day.

—ARIEL OVADIA

I'm drawn to fabrics that demand experimentation.

—JEN KAO

Hand-loomed cotton and silk

—BIBHU MOHAPATRA

Leather and crystals

—CHERYL FINNEGAN

Leather. I like leather very much because it is a skin. It breathes, it reacts to the body, and it works very well as a trim. I find it very inspirational from the touch to the aesthetic—giving it that rock 'n' roll feel.

—YIGAL AZROUËL

Any material with a personality that calls for taming

—DEVI KROELL

Chiffon, lace, tulle, and gauze

—ERIN FETHERSTON

Merino wool

—GABRIELA PEREZUTTI

Cottons and fine wool

—HENRY GRETHEL

My favorite fabric to work with would be matte jersey.

—DAVID MEISTER

Jerseys. They are the foundation to what we do.

—JEFFREY COSTELLO

Silk chiffon

—GILLES MENDEL

Fine wool crepe from Italy with a minimum of 5 percent Lycra in dense, beautiful colors

—KAY UNGER

Gray flannel. I think the only thing I wouldn't like in gray flannel is a bathing suit—and honestly it would look so chic, but be so silly.

—JENNA LYONS

Organic cotton
—JOHN PATRICK

Heavy wool
—STEVEN COX

Guipure lace
—LELA ROSE

Silk wool
—PAMELLA ROLAND

Knits
—LIZ LANGE

Ebony wool
—PATRICIA VON MUSULIN

Cotton oxford cloth shirting
—SCOTT STERNBERG

Beaded silk
—STACEY BENDET

Cashmere in all its iterations
—STAN HERMAN

Cashmere, silk, and lace
—KOI SUWANNAGATE

Leather
—REBECCA MINKOFF

Stretch denim jeans
—ROBERT LEE MORRIS

Cashmere
—SHANE BAUM

Denim
—SIMON ALCANTARA

Embroidered silks
—KEREN CRAIG

Cotton jersey
—NATALIE CHANIN

We utilize a lot of tulle, organza, embroidery, and lace in our collections.
—GEORGINA CHAPMAN

Anything with color
—NICK GRAHAM

I am fascinated by the unique qualities of fossilized materials. The minerals in the earth and in the ocean change the color of the fossilized woolly mammoth ivory, fossilized walrus ivory, and fossilized dinosaur bone over tens of thousands of years creating one-of-a-kind rare hues. The more color that appears in a fossil, the more rare it is.
—MONIQUE PÉAN

A good coat. It seems that there are a lot of events that you go to in New York where people mainly just see you in your coat, no matter how much time you spent on your outfit.

—ANNA SUI

A pair of men's classic black loafers

—AMY SMILOVIC

The perfect date dress

—BIBHU MOHAPATRA

A flirty dress

—CHARLOTTE RONSON

A white shirt

—CAROLINA HERRERA

A draped dress

—ROBERT TAGLIAPIETRA

A man's watch

—MICHAEL BASTIAN

A great little black dress . . . and lots of diamonds

—DAVID MEISTER

A great pair of hoops

—MELISSA JOY MANNING

A white shirt (preferably with monogram), great jeans, a perfect blazer, a good watch, a trench coat, simple black shoes, a cashmere sweater, and a really new toothbrush

—JENNA LYONS

Great jeans

—MICHAEL LEVA

EVERY WOMAN SHOULD OWN

A perfect pair of leather pants and a fitted, crisp, white men's shirt

—JENNIFER FISHER

Vintage. Style is so much more interesting when you mix old and new. To me, collecting vintage is like collecting art.

—BRIAN ATWOOD

A long evening dress to make her dream

—CATHERINE MALANDRINO

As many shoes as she can

—ULRICH GRIMM

Something that makes her feel long, lean, and leggy

—DONNA KARAN

A sexy black dress

—EDDIE RODRIGUEZ

An oversized masculine coat

—MARCELLA LINDEBERG

A trench coat

—GEMMA KAHNG

Something that makes her feel extraordinary every time she wears it

—JILL STUART

A few weird accessories to amp up simple wardrobe pieces

—LISA MAYOCK

The confidence to please herself

—GERARD YOSCA

A Sabbia Rosa slip

—IRENE NEUWIRTH

A black leather jacket
—YIGAL AZROUËL

An impeccable white
shirt and a pair of
beaten-up jeans
—MICHAEL SMALDONE

The perfect LBD
—MICHELLE OCHS

A pair of killer stilettos
—ALEXANDRE BIRMAN

A men's shirt
—ERIN BEATTY

Silk pajamas
—NANETTE LEPORE

Great jewelry—real or
fake. Another essential is
a cashmere cape. When
you can't get a coat
to work over certain
outfits it's the perfect
answer, especially in the
evening—it doesn't even
have to be checked.
—MARY ANN RESTIVO

A red dress
—PRABAL GURUNG

An agenda,
almost worn-out,
from Hermès
—RALPH RUCCI

A good pair of shoes
TABITHA SIMMONS

A classic handbag
in an exotic skin
—REED KRAKOFF

Robert Lee
Morris silver
heart pendants
—ROBERT LEE MORRIS

A little black dress

—MAGGIE NORRIS

A great pea coat
—VERA WANG

I'm into the extra
layer that really makes
the look, so I'd say a
killer slim-cut dress,
a leather jacket that
fits like a glove, and
a statement coat in a
bold color that turns
heads and never gets
lost in a pile at a party.
—MICHELLE SMITH

Feminine versions of
classic menswear
—SHIMON OVADIA

A classic black dress
and a fitted blazer
to wear over it
—PAMELLA ROLAND

Cat Eye sunglasses
—PATTY PERREIRA

A very good bag and
a very good watch
—PETER SOM

Her own style.
Confidence is everything.
—SHAUN KEARNEY

A great jacket to enhance
and transform
—SHELLY STEFFEE

A vintage car
—TRINA TURK

A large three-way mirror
—PATRICIA VON MUSULIN

A Swiss Army Knife
—YEOHLEE TENG

Chic heels she can wear all day and a bag that can go from day to night

—MONICA BOTKIER

Fake eyelashes and sexy unders

—BETSEY JOHNSON

A perfect pair of chic black sunglasses

—CHRISTIAN ROTH

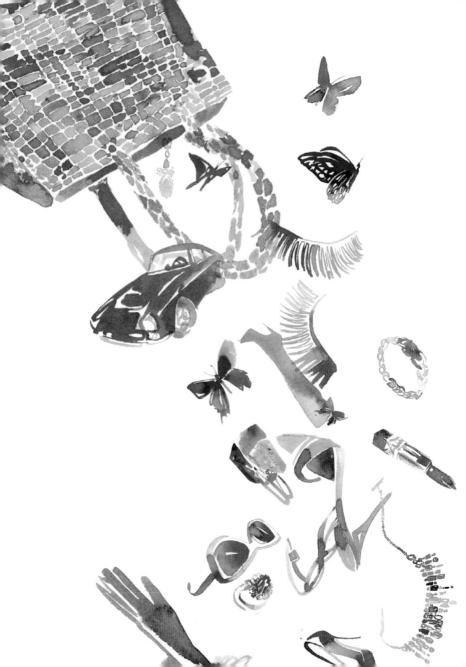

A pair of beat-up Levi's
—AMY SMILOVIC

A signature style
—ARIEL OVADIA

A tux, a good watch,
and a gym membership
—BRIAN ATWOOD

A silk scarf
—CATHERINE MALANDRINO

A classic double-
breasted coat
—MARCELLA LINDEBERG

A sexy black suit
—EDDIE RODRIGUEZ

A fedora hat
—GEMMA KAHNG

A good tuxedo
—LUBOV AZRIA

The finest lightweight
wool, darkest midnight-
blue tuxedo with notched
collar and no vest
—KAY UNGER

His own tuxedo
—MARY ANN RESTIVO

In my dream world,
every man owns a
tuxedo-printed T-shirt.
—LISA MAYOCK

A leather jacket
—MICHAEL LEVA

A stylish cuff link
—MELISSA JOY MANNING

An impeccable white
shirt and a pair of
beaten-up jeans
—MICHAEL SMALDONE

EVERY MAN SHOULD OWN

A leather jacket
—CHARLOTTE RONSON

A plaid shirt
—ROBERT TAGLIAPIETRA

A fabulous leather jacket
—DAVID MEISTER

A horse
—DAVID YURMAN

A vintage watch
—DEBORAH LLOYD

A navy blazer
—DENNIS BASSO

A white shirt (preferably
with monogram), great
jeans, a perfect blazer,
a good watch, a trench
coat, simple black shoes,
a cashmere sweater, and
a good nose-hair clipper
—JENNA LYONS

A great umbrella
from James Smith
in London
—KEANAN DUFFTY

A perfectly tailored suit
—JEFF HALMOS

Silk pajamas
—NANETTE LEPORE

A pink oxford button-
down shirt for days
you're hungover or
just feeling under the
weather. Trust me on
this one.
—MICHAEL BASTIAN

A large three-way
mirror
—PATRICIA VON MUSULIN

The Perfect Aviator
—PATTY PERREIRA

A Swiss Army Knife

—YEOHLEE TENG

A perfectly tailored tux, and wear it as often as possible

—RACHEL DOOLEY

A custom suit

—REED KRAKOFF

Robert Lee Morris silver cross link bracelets

—ROBERT LEE MORRIS

A tuxedo

—CHRISTIAN ROTH

A good tailored suit that fits well. Nothing worse than an ill-fitted suit on a bloke.

—SHAUN KEARNEY

A leather jacket. A worn pair of jeans he bought new. A tuxedo.

—SHIMON OVADIA

Incredible cuff links

—TRINA TURK

A navy suit and a good pair of boots

—BILLY REID

A watch that will last three generations

—DAO-YI CHOW

A very good pair of shoes and a very good watch

—PETER SOM

A fantastic watch

—PRABAL GURUNG

As many shoes as he can

—ULRICH GRIMM

A great pea coat

—VERA WANG

De Vera (if I can afford it one day!)

—ALBERTUS SWANEPOEL

Fairway Market in
Red Hook, Brooklyn

—ARAKS YERAMYAN

I always feel a romance for the past. Going to the flea market
is like taking a trip on a magic carpet to exotic places and times.
I want to visit the flea market in every city I visit.

—ANNA SUI

Anywhere with a lot of clutter

—PATRICIA VON MUSULIN

MY FAVORITE PLACE TO SHOP IS

Any Duane Reade

—MICHAEL BASTIAN

Les Marchés de Provence

—CATHERINE MALANDRINO

Flea markets in small towns

—GEMMA KAHNG

Hong Kong for custom-tailored suits, pants, and shirts

—CHRISTIAN ROTH

A place with stores.
I don't discriminate—
if there is a
register, then I'm in!

—JENNA LYONS

Online

—JENNIFER FISHER

Portobello Road

—JILL STUART

Nepenthes, NY

—DAIKI SUZUKI

Discovering local artisans in whichever part of the world I happen to visit: I always love their passion and discovering local customs.

—DEVI KROELL

Online

—JENNIFER MEYER

Capitol—Charlotte, North Carolina

—IRENE NEUWIRTH

The Salvation Army

—LAUREN MOFFATT

Tokyo

—ITALO ZUCCHELLI

eBay for vintage finds

—RACHEL DOOLEY

Muji

—SCOTT STERNBERG

In my sample room

—RACHEL ROY

The Paris Flea Market of Saint-Ouen

—SANG A IM-PROPP

I want to visit a flea market in every city I visit.

—ANNA SUI

The Late Lamented Old England in Paris

—JEFFREY BANKS

The ck Calvin Klein stores in Asia. The fit and cut of the clothes sold there are perfect for my proportion and size.

—KEVIN CARRIGAN

Brazil

—NICOLE MILLER

Daikanyama Tokyo. You find the most incredible things on these little hidden streets.

—SHAUN KEARNEY

It's a form of
self respect.

—DEVI KROELL

It's a compelling form
of self-expression.

—DANIELLE SNYDER

It is what
I do.

—DIANE VON FURSTENBERG

Fashion is a necessity in your
everyday life even if you don't
think it is. I have a passion
for fashion. I love that fashion
is a fantasy. Its madness is a
mystery and it's fun.

—CAROLINA HERRERA

If understood
properly,
it makes you
relevant!

—SAL CESARANI

FASHION IS IMPORTANT TO ME BECAUSE

It can change your mood, it can
instantly have someone feel
beautiful. . . . It's better than a pill.

—ARAKS YERAMYAN

As my work,
it is what I
choose to express
my ideas about
culture

—DEREK LAM

It is the ultimate daily
form of self-expression

—LISA SALZER

Fashion is worn by
all and has great
cultural and social
significance.

—MARIA SNYDER

It is always an unconscious
marker of history.

—ROLAND NIVELAIS

It's my life.
—BETSEY JOHNSON

It helps me express myself creatively.
—RON CHERESKIN

It is the first and last defining thing you present to people when you meet them.
—ROBERT TAGLIAPIETRA

Fashion is worn by all.
—MARIA SNYDER

It's creative and expressive.
—DONNA KARAN

I'm able to make women feel beautiful.
—ELIE TAHARI

Personal style reveals something internal about a person that is often hard to verbalize.
—FLORA GILL

It's disappearing, and that worries me.
—CAROLINA AMATO

It is my favorite form of communication.
—JAMES PURCELL

It supports my lifestyle.
—JEFF HALMOS

It is an expression of society and reflects back to us what we envision our culture to be about.
—JOHN BARTLETT

It defines a period in time.
—KENNETH BONAVITACOLA

It's a part of our culture of a giving place. Ultimately it is a form of communication.
—KOI SUWANNAGATE

It's an art form we can wear.
—LAURIE LYNN STARK

Without it, the world would be quite a scary place.
—LISA JENKS

It is an *enabler* . . . both mentally and physically.
—LUIS FERNANDEZ

It provides a voice and a way to stand out in the world and a way to tell your visual story.
—MARA HOFFMAN

It's how you put yourself out in the world. It gives you confidence.
—MARIA CORNEJO

It is in my DNA.
—MARY ANN RESTIVO

It's my passion. Ever since I was a kid, I was sketching ballerinas on the kitchen floor—passion has always been my first love.
—MICHELLE SMITH

It is the lifeblood to my soul.
—VANESSA NOEL

I feel connected to the world through the artistry of their work. It's a form of expression, and what we choose to wear communicates our individuality.
—MIMI SO

There is an immense amount of creativity that goes into a designer's work. There is fantasy and the reality of function. This is a wonderful equation to solve over and over again.
—MONICA BOTKIER

It's a form of expression. You can learn so much about someone from the way they present themselves.
—PAMELLA ROLAND

It is a visual hint of the psyche.
—SHELLY STEFFEE

It lets you define yourself from the inside out without saying a word.
—RACHEL ROY

It fuels my creativity and it's always on the move.
—RAFE TOTENGCO

It is how we present ourselves to the world. Fashion speaks before the person does in most cases.
—R. SCOTT FRENCH

It's the filter through which I express ideas to the world.
—SCOTT STERNBERG

It can be a form of nonverbal expression.
—SIMON ALCANTARA

Style is at an individual's core; trend is just a fleeting magazine cover (or blog post).
—AMY SMILOVIC

Style is a thread that you take with you and can work trends into.
—ARAKS YERAMYAN

Style is personal and trends are business.
—BETSEY JOHNSON

Style is a personal choice. Trends are someone else's choice for you.
—CHARLOTTE RONSON

Style is a perspective, trends are marketing tools.
—JEFFREY COSTELLO

Trends you look like other people. Style you look like a better version of yourself.
—CYNTHIA ROWLEY

Taste
—EDDIE BORGO

Style is intrinsic, trends are of the moment.
—GEORGINA CHAPMAN

Style must be developed over years and changed to suit oneself as they grow older and wiser. Trends are of the moment and sometimes work, sometimes not.
—ISAAC MANEVITZ

Style is an attitude; a trend is just another thing to follow.
—LELA ROSE

THE DIFFERENCE BETWEEN STYLE AND TRENDS IS

Someone who is finding out who they are follows trends and someone who knows who they are has style
—NORMA KAMALI

Style is a personal expression of who you are; trends are the collective expressions of others.
—BLAKE KUWAHARA

Originality vs. copying
—JAMES PURCELL

"Style" is a cliché and "trend" is a cliché that changes more regularly.
—KEANAN DUFFTY

Style is innate and timeless—it cannot be bought. A trend is something of the moment that can be purchased.
—DAVID MEISTER

Style is a part of you, trends are something you wear.
—DONNA KARAN

Style is a personal expression, and trends are reflections of what our culture is embracing in the moment.
—JOHN BARTLETT

Style is quiet and trend is loud.
—JOHN PATRICK

Style is individual, trend is a moment.
—SHELLY STEFFEE

Trend is a hibiscus frosted donut; style is a seven-layer chocolate cake.
—LISA JENKS

Style is forever, and trends come and go. Anyone can adapt a trend. Style is innate.
—LIZ LANGE

Style never changes.
—RALPH RUCCI

Longevity
—EDDIE RODRIGUEZ

Trends represent the collective statement of a moment or generation while style is a constant.
—MONICA BOTKIER

Style is cultivated; trends are followed.
—REED KRAKOFF

Simply what remains in your closet more than a season. If your entire closet changes

a trend is just someone you had dinner with.
—NICK GRAHAM

Style is philosophy and trends are a nuisance.
—PRABAL GURUNG

Style is eternal, trends come and go.
—BIBHU MOHAPATRA

Style is a personal projection while trend is an abstract concept

personality!

—ROLAND NIVELAIS

Style is innate, inherent, and forever. Trend is Hello . . . Good-bye.
—LOUIS DELL'OLIO

Real style is a gift. Trends are a—moment—and not always a good one.
—MICHAEL BASTIAN

What separates the leaders and the followers.
—MIMI SO

every season, I hope that you are twelve and going through a growth spurt. Otherwise, you may not yet know who you are.
—NATALIE CHANIN

Trend is what you buy. Style is what you do with it.
—RAFE TOTENGCO

Style is like knowing someone all your life;

that is connected with fast-changing moods and fleeting thoughts.
—ROBERT LEE MORRIS

Style can't be taught. It's in the nature of a person. Trends are easily accessible and they fade.
—SHIMON OVADIA

Style is about what works well on you; trend is about fitting in.
—SIMON ALCANTARA

No rules
—**ADRIENNE LANDAU**

Less is more except when more is more.
—**BLAKE KUWAHARA**

If you love it, then you can work it.
—**ERICA COURTNEY**

Always wear clothes that fit and compliment.
—**HENRY GRETHEL**

Aesthetic is subjective . . . craftsmanship is objective.
—**JONATHAN MEIZLER**

Always dress up rather than down and never get rid of great evening pieces. You'd be surprised at how right they can look when used in a clever new way.
—**MARY ANN RESTIVO**

Know who you are
—**YEOHLEE TENG**

When you find something you love, buy it in all colors and two in black.
—**PATTY PERREIRA**

Don't take it all too seriously; a little something off keeps things fresh.
—**RACHEL DOOLEY**

You don't need money to have style.
—**RACHEL ZOE**

MY FASHION MOTTO IS

Never underestimate the power of perception.
—**JAMES PURCELL**

Wear what you love. Wear what feels good.
—**JOSIE NATORI**

Confuse and amuse. I am a firm believer that you should always try to wear something that makes no sense with the rest of your outfit, and something that's funny.
—**LISA MAYOCK**

If it ain't comfortable, don't wear it!
—**MONICA BOTKIER**

I hate this: "Before you go out, turn in to the mirror and whatever it is you notice, take it off." I'd say this: "Before you go out, turn in to the mirror and whatever it is you notice, put more of it on."
—**NICK GRAHAM**

Push one step further but reduce, simplify, and always have integrity.
—**RALPH RUCCI**

Always seek the one item that becomes your signature piece and defines your personal philosophy.
—**ROBERT LEE MORRIS**

A kick in the butt is good, if you're facing the right direction.
—**ELIE TAHARI**

Greatness is
in the details.

—R. SCOTT FRENCH

Accentuate the
positive, delete
the negative.

—DONNA KARAN

When in doubt,
go luxe. There's
nothing more stylish
than confidence.

—ROD KEENAN

Have fun	ADRIENNE LANDAU	Be dull
Less	AMY SMILOVIC	More
Carry a bag. Wear earrings. Keep things simple.	ARAKS YERAMYAN	Wear a trend if it doesn't have you looking amazing and beautiful.
Buy quality	BARRY BRICKEN	Buy cheap
Wear what you want and be you	BETSEY JOHNSON	Fake it
Wear good shoes	BLAKE KUWAHARA	Wear toe rings
Be confident in what you wear	BRADLEY BAYOU	Overdo it

ALWAYS		NEVER
Wear sunglasses	CAROLE HOCHMAN	Wear shorts
Reveal your assets and never forgive your weaknesses	CATHERINE MALANDRINO	Do the reverse!
Be confident in what you are wearing	CHARLOTTE RONSON	Try too hard
Stay true to your style and your age	CHERYL FINNEGAN	Fall for a trend that is not age appropriate
Look the part and feel comfortable	CHRISTIAN ROTH	Overdress
Mix plaids and patterns	COSTELLO TAGLIAPIETRA	Wear something that doesn't make you happy

ALWAYS

Be you

NEVER

Force it

—DIANE VON FURSTENBERG

ALWAYS		NEVER
Be yourself	DANIEL SILVER	Try too hard
Be manicured	DENNIS BASSO	Try to dress too young
Be true to yourself	DOUGLAS HANNANT	Look around and follow
Confident	EDDIE RODRIGUEZ	Presumptuous
Heels	ERICA COURTNEY	Flats
Stay true to your vision	ERIN FETHERSTON	Chase trends
Strive for quality	GABRIELA PEREZUTTI	Believe the hype
Have fun	GEORGINA CHAPMAN	Limit yourself
Try	GILLES MENDEL	Try too hard
Dress appropriately to the occasion	HENRY JACOBSON	Wear a tracksuit for anything but exercise

ALWAYS		NEVER
Be yourself and not be afraid to wear big jewelry	ISAAC MANEVITZ	Leave the house without accessorizing
Behave	JOHN PATRICK	Clash
Be curious	JONATHAN MEIZLER	Be afraid to make mistakes
Save your favorites	JUDITH RIPKA	Say never
Wear too many bangles	KAY UNGER	Go without a beautiful handkerchief in your bag or pocket
Be comfortable	KENNETH BONAVITACOLA	Judge the fashion choices of others

ALWAYS

RSVP

NEVER

Crash the party

—KEANAN DUFFTY

ALWAYS		NEVER
Experiment	KEREN CRAIG	Follow rules
Buy a few designer's brand pieces that you loved every season	KOI SUWANNAGATE	Forget about proportions
Be bold	L'WREN SCOTT	Compromise
Wear what you feel like yourself in	LAUREN MOFFATT	Look like you tried too hard
Dress with confidence	LAURIE LYNN STARK	Dress because you think it's how you should
Be elegant	MICHEL KRAMER-METRAUX	Be disheveled
Wear clothing that flatters your shape	LIZ LANGE	Blindly follow trends

ALWAYS   **NEVER**

ALWAYS		NEVER
Be honest	LOUIS DELL'OLIO	Be phony
Take risks	LUBOV AZRIA	Doubt yourself
Dress for yourself	MARTIN COOPER	Let anyone decide it for you
Accessorize	MELISSA JOY MANNING	Leave the house without mascara
Try	MICHAEL LEVA	Try too hard
Stay true	MICHAEL SMALDONE	Complicate
Be elegant	MICHEL KRAMER-METRAUX	Be disheveled
Wear color	MICHELLE SMITH	Squeeze into anything—if it's too tight, go a size up!

ALWAYS

Listen to your own inner voice

NEVER

Rely on what people think

—MARCELLA LINDEBERG

Wear something you feel confident in	MONICA BOTKIER	Wear something just because everyone else is
Wear your jewelry	MONICA RICH KOSANN	Keep it locked up
Take risks	NANETTE LEPORE	Say never
Lead	NICK GRAHAM	Follow
Play honest	OLIVIER THEYSKENS	Lose integrity
Have fun with what you wear	PAMELA LOVE	Look uncomfortable
Dress for yourself	PAMELLA ROLAND	Try to impress anyone else
Do your own thing	PATRICIA VON MUSULIN	Follow anyone
Chic and sexy	PRABAL GURUNG	TTH [try too hard]

ALWAYS		**NEVER**
Take risks	RACHEL ZOE	Wear too many trends at one time
Have fun	RAFE TOTENGCO	Take yourself too seriously
Be kind	RALPH RUCCI	Flash
Explore your individuality	VERA WANG	Dress like others
Wear something that makes you a bit uncomfortable	REBECCA MINKOFF	Wear too tight of a shoe, you will limp all day
Your own	REBECCA TAYLOR	Forced
Be yourself	REEM ACRA	Try to be anything else

ALWAYS		NEVER
Be yourself	ROBERT RODRIGUEZ	Be a fashion victim
Be comfortable and loose	ROBERT LEE MORRIS	Be bound and struggling with what you are wearing just for the fashion moment
Trust your gut	ROD KEENAN	Be a fashion victim
Classic	SCOTT STERNBERG	Staid
Wear high heels and sunglasses	SELIMA SALAUN	Wear crocs
Err on the side of history	SHANE BAUM	Try too hard
Dress for yourself and no one else. Own it.	SHAUN KEARNEY	Dress for your ego but for your heart and soul

ALWAYS	**NEVER**

ALWAYS		NEVER
Individual	SHELLY STEFFEE	Conformist
Feel comfortable in what you wear; it will automatically give you confidence.	SHIMON OVADIA	Follow the crowd
Be well mannered	SIMON ALCANTARA	Be rude
Less	SOPHIE BUHAI	More
Smile	STAN HERMAN	Frown
Be yourself	STEPHEN BURROWS	Wear white stockings, unless a nurse

ALWAYS

Follow your gut

NEVER

Lose your head

—GILLES MENDEL

ALWAYS

Trust your
instincts

NEVER

Follow
trends

—ZAC POSEN

ALWAYS		NEVER
Brush your teeth	STEVEN COX	Shout at someone
Keep an open mind	TRINA TURK	Say never
Pair confidence with graciousness	WARIS AHLUWALIA	Forget kindness is always in style
Experiment	YIGAL AZROUËL	Hide
Wear clothes that support your personal image	STEFAN MILJANIC	Let the clothes overwhelm your personality
Think about the next thing	ADRIANO GOLDSCHMIED	Just be satisfied in your success
Look relaxed	DEREK LAM	Wear something itchy

ALWAYS   **NEVER**

ALWAYS		NEVER
Stick to classic cuts and silhouettes, and don't be afraid to play with new patterns and bold pops of color	TOMMY HILFIGER	Fall victim to too many trends; it is tempting, but when you do that you lose your identity and that is what is most important to your brand

career

I put on my mother's
fur coat at five and
refused to take it off
—ADRIENNE LANDAU

I got my first *Vogue*
subscription, at nine
—ARAKS YERAMYAN

My father took me to
NYC to buy his fabrics
when I was five years old
—BARRY BRICKEN

I hit NYC in 1964
—BETSEY JOHNSON

My father offered
me a pair of Ray Ban
sunglasses at age
fifteen (in 1974, when
they were not available
yet in Europe)
—CHRISTIAN ROTH

I saw Cher on TV
—DAVID MEISTER

I started making
dresses
—DIANE VON
FURSTENBERG

I learned about great
designers from a lecture
on "history of fashion"
at the School of the Art
Institute of Chicago
—GEMMA KAHNG

I went to the
Victoria and Albert
Museum as a child
—GEORGINA CHAPMAN

I was a young child,
helping my father
in his atelier
—GILLES MENDEL

I KNEW I WANTED TO BE A DESIGNER WHEN

I put on my first fashion
show at sixteen years old.
I turned the dining-room
table into a stage and my
sisters were my models.
It got rave reviews!
—BRIAN ATWOOD

At eight everyone was
looking at me because
I dressed so differently
and then I realized the
power of clothes
—CATHERINE MALANDRINO

I saw the Disney
Cinderella movie
around six years old.
After watching the
scene of the birds
and mice putting
together a dress for
Cinderella, I ran to my
grandmother's closet
and started cutting
her lace silk sleeping
gowns to make the
same dress.
—GABRIELA PEREZUTTI

I figured out I could
mold metal and use
my sculptor skills to
make jewelry
—ISAAC MANEVITZ

My sister home-
sewed a bad shift
dress in 1969
—JAMES PURCELL

I reworked my school
uniform every day
—JOHN BARTLETT

I started designing clothes inspired by my favorite rock-'n'-roll icons

—TOMMY HILFIGER

I traveled to London in 1964 and saw that every rule in fashion, music, and culture had been broken.

—NORMA KAMALI

I fell in love with figure skating and designed my own costume

—VERA WANG

I looked at a garment and sketched a way to improve it

—MAXWELL OSBORNE

I wanted to design things I was missing

—TORY BURCH

Always. It is part of my DNA.

—JUDITH RIPKA

I saw Shirley MacLaine wearing Edith Head's extraordinary costumes in the film *What a Way to Go!*

—KENNETH BONAVITACOLA

I knew exactly what I wanted to wear, but I couldn't find it at the mall

—LAUREN MOFFATT

I spent a high school summer at Parsons School of Design in NYC

—LISA JENKS

Always. I would design and create couture for my dolls when I was a child.

—MAGGIE NORRIS

I saw YSL's 1977 Russian Peasant Collection

—MICHAEL LEVA

While I was working in finance when I began my career out of college, my younger sister Vanessa Péan passed away in a car accident at the age of sixteen. At that moment, I realized it was necessary for me to reevaluate what I wanted to do with my life. My sister's desire to help others at such a young age inspired me to find a way to fuse my love for art, design, and philanthropy.

—MONIQUE PÉAN

I was ten years old

—NANETTE LEPORE

My family knew I wanted to be a designer when I would show up to Sunday lunch in vintage prom dresses and a tiara from my grandmother's attic closet. I've always had my own style, even if I haven't always had my own tiara.

—NATALIE CHANIN

I started designing my own clothes in fifth grade

—RAFE TOTENGCO

I've always known . . . it felt like a very natural transition from being a stylist. I needed to wait until I had the time to give to it.

—RACHEL ZOE

I was eight years old and making quilts with my grandmother

—R. SCOTT FRENCH

I realized what the job actually was day to day

—SCOTT STERNBERG

I opened my first store (as an optician and optometrist) and could not find the essential pieces I loved on the market

—SELIMA SALAUN

I couldn't find what I wanted on the shelves and assumed there must be a few others who felt like me

—SHANE BAUM

I looked at the pattern books in my father's silk shops

—STAN HERMAN

Studying art I entered a world fashion competition and won. I had no idea that I was that good at it. I thought I wanted to be an architect.

—SHAUN KEARNEY

I finished looking through a rare, ca. 1925, British fashion publication at the age of ten. The magazine paper was out of this world, the images inside were projecting importance and happiness . . . and the freedom of expression in that magazine projected the world that I wanted to travel to.

—STEFAN MILJANIC

ca. 1961

—STEPHEN BURROWS

Since I was five. I used to draw pictures of women and clothes, even writing out all the measurements.

—TESS GIBERSON

I used to help style my mum when I was young

—DAVID NEVILLE

70

I watched my sister change from her Catholic school uniform to a miniskirt, platforms, and silver glitter eyeshadow as she left the driveway

—MICHAEL SMALDONE

Someone told
me that it was
an actual job
to create clothes

—OLIVIER THEYSKENS

Have a distinct
vision for your
brand and always
stay true to your
core values

—TOMMY HILFIGER

Know what you love

—ERIN BEATTY

Love it!

—BETSEY JOHNSON

Try to survive and be
as current as possible

—SAL CESARANI

Be obsessed,
passionate,
and love every
minute of it

—ADRIENNE LANDAU

Persevere

—ALBERTUS SWANEPOEL

TO MAKE IT IN FASHION, YOU MUST

Have balls
of steel and
never give up

—ERICA COURTNEY

Find a space to
balance craft,
imagination, and
pragmatism.

—DEREK LAM

Have a thick skin and
passion for the craft

—BIBHU MOHAPATRA

Have perseverance,
discipline, and talent

—CAROLINA HERRERA

Be different, have a creative vision,
follow your agenda, and work hard

—CHRISTIAN ROTH

Be relentless

—NANETTE LEPORE

Never give up

—MAXWELL OSBORNE

Love it. Keep your
eye on the prize.

—AMY CHAN

Stick to your guns,
but be open to
compromise

—JEFFREY BANKS

Have a vision and
believe in it

—DONNA KARAN

Make your customers,
mentors, press,
stores, employees,
and even factories
root for your success

—FLORA GILL

Know how to read
a balance sheet

—JEFF HALMOS

Constantly challenge
yourself, both
creatively and otherwise

—GEORGINA CHAPMAN

Be thoughtful

—EDDIE BORGO

Toughen up,
thicken the skin,
and be fearless

—LOUIS DELL'OLIO

Keep your ideas
50,000 feet above
and your feet
on the ground

—MICHAEL SMALDONE

Work Work Work

—DANIEL SILVER

Know who you're
dressing and where
she's wearing it

—DOUGLAS HANNANT

Be patient

—LUIS FERNANDEZ

Never take no
for an answer

—NARCISO RODRIGUEZ

Have good
business instincts

—MARY McFADDEN

Be resilient

—NICOLE MILLER

Have a point of
view that you're
willing to die for

—DAO-YI CHOW

Be tenacious

—CYNTHIA VINCENT

Have distinct
vision and a passion
for that vision

—KARA ROSS

Have a good head
on your shoulders

—MICHELLE OCHS

Have indefatigable
drive and talent.
Never stop believing
in yourself.

—MICHELLE SMITH

Love what you
start out to do and
still love it every
step of the way

—STEPHEN DWECK

Realize your creativity but live in reality. It is not an easy business and you have to fight hard to break in. Once you get some encouragement don't sit on it, build on it!

—MONICA BOTKIER

Check your ego

—PRABAL GURUNG

Have thick skin and be persistent

—RACHEL ZOE

Never lose your humility

—RALPH RUCCI

Be willing to live and breathe the business and be willing to be criticized

—R. SCOTT FRENCH

Work hard and be fearless in creativity

—SELIMA SALAUN

Want to be in fashion more than anything else

—MONIKA TILLEY

Have a very clear vision of who you want to dress, and why no one else is making clothing for her

—SOPHIE BUHAI

Be prolific, trust your instincts, be patient, and master your craft

—SIMON ALCANTARA

Be yourself

—NICK GRAHAM

Play the game while trying to retain your integrity

—STAN HERMAN

Love what you do, have a distinct point of view, and have a smart business partner to help you execute that vision

—RAFE TOTENGCO

Create like a madman, execute like a businessman

—SHELLY STEFFEE

In addition to talent, one must be extraordinarily bold and lucky. It doesn't hurt if one possesses the skills of a successful businessman, artist, inventor, constructor, politician, and marketer.

—STEFAN MILJANIC

When your designs
start to influence others
—ADRIANO GOLDSCHMIED

Let you know
when we
get there
—MAXWELL OSBORNE

Being able to smile
and reach for more
challenges after
each gamble on
the unknown,
on the future
—JOAN HELPERN

Balancing career and
personal life equally
—CAROLINA AMATO

Loving what you do
at least 50 percent of the time
and keeping a roof over
the heads of all involved
—GERARD YOSCA

I DEFINE SUCCESS AS

Perfecting your personal vision
—VERA WANG

Not giving
a damn
what any-
one thinks
—KEANAN DUFFTY

When women
tell me how
beautiful they feel
in my clothes
—ARAKS YERAMYAN

Security, happiness,
and most of all health!
—SAL CESARANI

Doing what I love to do
—AMY CHAN

Enjoying what you do and seeing other people happy that you've done it
—MARY ANN RESTIVO

Vision with integrity
—MARY PING

Fanatically doing what you think is right
—MICHAEL SMALDONE

Evolving from a designer into a brand that stands for something. Seeing women on the street enjoying my designs in a practical way. Celebration of the modern woman!
—MONICA BOTKIER

Looking forward to going to work every day
—R. SCOTT FRENCH

Personally, success is having a happy and healthy family; professionally, success is having a collection women covet.
—RACHEL ZOE

Finding happiness in what you make and do
—STACEY BENDET

The full realization of an idea, from concept to consumer, with integrity and quality intact
—SCOTT STERNBERG

Loving what you do
—STEVEN COX

Loving what you do and being appreciated for it
—SELIMA SALAUN

Know what you
are not good at

—BIBHU MOHAPATRA

Have your own
clear vision

—BLAKE KUWAHARA

Think like an
entrepreneur

—CYNTHIA ROWLEY

Be disciplined. Only
if one masters the basics
can one truly excel.

—DEVI KROELL

Always be
willing to learn

—KENNETH BONAVITACOLA

Have vision, strength,
and conviction. You
need a complete
understanding of your
craft, perseverance, and
openness to listen and
learn. A responsibility
to the business,
communication,
and integrity are
also important.

—KEVIN CARRIGAN

Be prepared to get
your hands dirty

—LUIS FERNANDEZ

Enjoy what you
do and not be fearful
of challenges

—SELIMA SALAUN

Surround yourself
with people much
smarter then you and
be willing to work
harder than you
ever imagined

—RACHEL ROY

IN ORDER TO BE SUCCESSFUL AT WORK, YOU SHOULD

For me, it is traveling,
relating to your
customers, working
hard, and having
good manners.

—IRENE NEUWIRTH

Work hard and be
open to ideas

—JILL STUART

Always evolve,
always innovate

—JOSIE NATORI

Work hard, be kind

—REBECCA TAYLOR

My father always told
me that if I want to
have my own company,
I should be in the office
everyday before the rest
of my staff—and stay
later than anyone else.
That philosophy of hard
work and dedication
has always inspired me.

—ANNA SUI

Ask questions,
and communicate

—LUBOV AZRIA

Have all of the qualities
that everyone has
already listed in this
book, with the addition
of two pieces: have
international experience
and speak at least one
additional language

—MARTIN COOPER

Always be organized

—MICHELLE OCHS

Understand the
importance of team

—PRABAL GURUNG

Fight for your ideas
—ADRIANO GOLDSCHMIED

Be willing to go beyond
what is expected to give others
what they weren't expecting
—ALEXA ADAMS

Surround yourself with talented people with a sense of humor
—MARY ANN RESTIVO

Have an open mind to
your employees and never be
afraid to fail. Be fearless in
your goals even if they don't
work out the way you planned.
Nothing ever really does
—CHRISTIAN SIRIANO

Never confuse confidence for arrogance
—PETER SOM

Meditate and drink soy lattes
—MARA HOFFMAN

Constantly challenge yourself
—JODIE SNYDER

Be open to people's opinions that are different from yours
—LISA PERRY

Love what you are doing
—DENNIS BASSO

Work hard, be gracious, and, most importantly, do something you love
—MAX OSTERWEIS

They don't
have an ego

—AMY SMILOVIC

They stay true to themselves. Don't
take the temperature in
the room before you give your own
opinion. Believe in yourself.

—JUDITH RIPKA

They remain undeterred, dust
themselves off, and try again

—DEVI KROELL

They take initiative

—DONNA KARAN

They don't
follow the crowd

—CHARLOTTE RONSON

They have passion, intelligence,
a keen sense of humor, work hard,
have good manners, are kind to other
people, and give back to the world

—DAVID MEISTER

I'M IMPRESSED WITH SOMEONE IF

They can strike a
balance between
family/work, art/
commerce, and
structure/freedom

—CYNTHIA ROWLEY

They are acrobats or surgeons

—GABY BASORA

They are fearless

—GEORGINA CHAPMAN

They think outside their job description

—JENNA LYONS

They have confidence in
themselves and aren't afraid to
stand out from the pack

—ERIN FETHERSTON

They say what they
mean and mean
what they say

—RACHEL ROY

They admit to making a mistake

—LISA PERRY

They always answer their emails and return all phone calls

—LIZ LANGE

I receive a handwritten thank-you note

—LISA JENKS

They have the skill to anticipate. Fashion is a very sensory business and "feeling and sensing" the needs of others around you or the business at hand is the beacon which will guide you.

—MARTIN COOPER

I see them performing an act of kindness for someone else and they don't realize anyone's watching

—MICHAEL BASTIAN

They do what they believe in . . . without compromise

—SANG A IM-PROPP

They live for the moment

—RACHEL DOOLEY

They show consistency in their creative endeavors

—ROBERT LEE MORRIS

They have integrity

—SHANE BAUM

They look me straight in the eye

—STAN HERMAN

They take responsibility for their mistakes

—MELISSA JOY MANNING

They are a generous collaborator

—ZAC POSEN

They are humble

—JOSEPH ALTUZARRA

A game ranger
—ALBERTUS SWANEPOEL

An archaeologist,
exploring late
Roman history
—ALEXA ADAMS

A Rockette, florist,
or cupcake decorator
—BETSEY JOHNSON

A plastic surgeon
—DAVID MEISTER

A florist
—DEBORAH LLOYD

An engineer. I love
to figure out how
things work and
devise systems. There
are a lot of parallels
with fashion design
and technology/
architecture/industrial
design. In both,
limitations of a
material can force an
elegant solution.
—FLORA GILL

I would work in film.
—JOSEPH ALTUZARRA

A surgeon
—MARY PING

A sociologist
or professional
scuba diver
—MELISSA JOY MANNING

A costume designer
—MICHAEL SMALDONE

A writer
—PATRICIA VON MUSULIN

A gentleman farmer
—PETER SOM

IF I COULD HAVE ANY OTHER JOB, IT WOULD BE

I would run an animal
rescue and write
children's books.
—ERIN FETHERSTON

A teacher. I love
mentoring—sharing
my experiences and
knowledge with a
new generation of
designers.
—RAFE TOTENGCO

A children's science
fiction author
—JEN KAO

Chef! I love to cook
for my family.
—ISAAC MANEVITZ

A Hollywood agent
—JAMES PURCELL

A zoologist
—KEANAN DUFFTY

I would own a
homemade ice-
cream shop.
—LELA ROSE

A ballerina
—MAGGIE NORRIS

An astronaut
—RACHEL DOOLEY

A child psychiatrist.
I have always been
fascinated by the mind
and I love children.
—RACHEL ZOE

A dolphin researcher
—REBECCA TAYLOR

A tenor with a high C
—STAN HERMAN

A golf pro
—DAVID NEVILLE

Bookstore owner
—DEREK LAM

A naval architect designing private megayachts
—R. SCOTT FRENCH

An architect
—ROBERT RODRIGUEZ

A Chef
—NICOLE MILLER

A writer. Telling stories is what I do with clothes.
—ROLAND NIVELAIS

An organic farmer
—TESS GIBERSON

A frustrated interior decorator
—LUBOV AZRIA

Gardener, coffee-shop owner, photographer
—ROBERT GELLER

To work for the CIA. Or maybe I just watch too many episodes of *Homeland*. Oh and I do love a conspiracy theory.
—SHAUN KEARNEY

Between politics or vagabond
—WARIS AHLUWALIA

An astronomer . . . .someone who could design the interstellar future for the world
—STEFAN MILJANIC

Creativity is not
enough to be
successful

—ADRIANO GOLDSCHMIED

It doesn't really
matter what
other people think
of me

—DAVID MEISTER

Hesitation
is death

—GREG ARMAS

You must not be afraid to fail
and be able to turn all
criticism into constructive criticism
and learn from your mistakes

—ISAAC MANEVITZ

I WISH I KNEW THEN, THAT

It takes ten years
minimum to build a brand

—LISA PERRY

I should buy
shares in Apple

—MARCUS WAINWRIGHT

Social media would become
so important

—CHRISTIAN ROTH

It's OK to make a lot of mistakes,
if you learn from them

—JUDITH RIPKA

Life is full
of amazing
moments, be
open to seeing
them

—LELA ROSE

The ability to write would be so
important. In a world of emails,
texts, and content, it is so valuable to
communicate what you want to say.

—LUBOV AZRIA

Talent is not enough

—MARCELLA LINDEBERG

I should have taken courses in human psychology when I was at Parsons

—MARTIN COOPER

Life never gets easier; find the humor in today and breathe

—MELISSA JOY MANNING

The smallest moments in life can be the biggest inspiration

—SELIMA SALAUN

Don't believe in regrets, it only slows you down

—MONICA RICH KOSANN

You don't always have to do everything perfectly, you just have to do

—NATALIE CHANIN

Fear of failure is unnecessary, but failing sometimes is necessary

—NICK GRAHAM

Time passes quickly

—PATRICIA VON MUSULIN

I didn't have to rush, and to enjoy the early stages of my career more

—REBECCA MINKOFF

Time passes as fast as it does

—R. SCOTT FRENCH

Tequila causes hangovers!

—STACEY BENDET

Steve Jobs—but recast with a bit of empathy

—AMY SMILOVIC

President Carter

—CYNTHIA VINCENT

Donna Karan

—ROBERT TAGLIAPIETRA

Dries Van Noten

—JEN KAO

Mickey Drexler

—JENNA LYONS

Marlene Dietrich

—L'WREN SCOTT

Reed Krakoff for brand vision in accessories and DVF as a fierce woman in the world

DVF and Marc Jacobs

—RACHEL ZOE

Paul Smith. He has remained true to himself, independent, and successful in an era of brand conglomeration.

—RAFE TOTENGCO

One who appreciates talent

Diana Vreeland— bold and daring

—DIANE VON FURSTENBERG

Glenda Bailey

—GABRIELA PEREZUTTI

Madame Grès

—GILLES MENDEL

making a serious mark and supporting others

—MONICA BOTKIER

Sigmund Freud

—NANETTE LEPORE

Someone who gives you their perspective on something but doesn't apply their ultimate judgment on your decision

—NICK GRAHAM

and opens your eyes to new ideas

—ROD KEENAN

Ralph Lauren

—SCOTT STERNBERG

In the fashion world, it has to be Calvin Klein.

—STEFAN MILJANIC

The first Seventh on Sale
—DONNA KARAN

Becoming a member!
—DAVID MEISTER

Getting to meet and work with the artist Tauba Auerbach on a *Vogue* photo shoot
—ALEXA ADAMS

Going to China with the CFDA last year
—GEMMA KAHNG

Meeting Michael Kors while out for dinner with Lisa Smilor
—ROBERT TAGLIAPIETRA

Going to my first CFDA Fashion awards this year
—ARIEL OVADIA

MY FAVORITE CFDA MEMORY IS

Of course, winning the CFDA Swarovski Perry Ellis Award for Best Accessory Design in 2003
—BRIAN ATWOOD

Meeting Princess Diana backstage at Lincoln Center the year I won the Perry Ellis Award
—CYNTHIA ROWLEY

When Diane von Furstenberg was elected as president
—CATHERINE MALANDRINO

Judging the *Vogue*/CFDA Fashion Fund and winning the CFDA Lifetime Achievement Award
—VERA WANG

When Steven Kolb called me with the news that I was a new member of the CFDA—I said, "Are you sure?!"
—CHERYL FINNEGAN

Receiving the
Womenswear Designer
of the Year in 2004
and being honored with
the Geoffrey Beene
Lifetime Achievement
Award in 2008.
—CAROLINA HERRERA

Begging the CFDA
to help me stage our
first show, with
very little money
—EDDIE RODRIGUEZ

When I hosted the
CFDA's new member's
party in 2008, it was
great to be a part
of a magical night
for others
—ELIE TAHARI

Being part of the CFDA
Vogue Fashion Fund
was amazing. Just
having thirty minutes
alone with the judges
to ask questions and
hear stories is worth all
the hard work.
—FLORA GILL

Winning Best
Menswear Award
—JOHN BARTLETT

The two Womenswear
Designer of the Year
awards I received in
2006 and 2008
—FRANCISCO COSTA

Delivering the
gorgeous trunk to
the CFDA office
GABY BASORA

The first Seventh on
Sale. The fashion
community took a big
hit in the early days of
the AIDS epidemic. We
would not be powerless.
We would roll up our
sleeves as a family and
set to work.
—GERARD YOSCA

My first show in
the tents at Bryant
Park in 2000
—JONATHAN MEIZLER

Celebrating with
my team and loved ones
after winning
the CFDA/*Vogue*
Fashion Fund
—JOSEPH ALTUZARRA

Meeting Norman Norell
—RALPH LAUREN

Learning of my
election to the CFDA.
For me, it brought
a special kind of
validation to a
lifetime of work in
the industry I love.
There is nothing
more deeply rewarding
than validation
received from one's
peers. They are
the ones that truly
understand.
—HENRY JACOBSON

Opening night of
Seventh on Sale at
The Armory in 1995,
working the receiving
line between Anna
Wintour and Fern
Mallis. Fern was
resplendent in my
ballgown made of
100 yards of lime
silk tulle. It was a
magical night.
—JAMES PURCELL

The wonderful
dinners outside at
Bryant Park
—JOSIE NATORI

The day I was
accepted into the
CFDA and was
congratulated by
Bill Blass
—KENNETH
BONAVITACOLA

Going to the CFDA/
Vogue Fashion Fund
awards for the first
time and meeting my
future husband
—LISA MAYOCK

The fabulous party
Reed and Delphine
Krakoff threw at
their glamorous town
house for new CFDA
members the year
I was accepted into
the CFDA
—LIZ LANGE

Being one of four
chairpersons on the
CFDA board when
we started "Fashion
Targets Breast
Cancer." It was
launched at the White
House with Bill and
Hillary Clinton.
—LOUIS DELL'OLIO

When I went to lobby
for copyright rights for
fashion designers
—MARIA CORNEJO

Scholarship Committee
Portfolio Reviews
—MICHAEL LEVA

Accepting the CFDA/
Vogue Fashion Fund
Award from Alber
Elbaz. He is such an
inspiration to me!
—MONIQUE PÉAN

My nomination to the
CFDA by Perry Ellis
when he was president
—PATRICIA VON MUSULIN

The first day as part
of the CFDA Fashion
Incubator, where I met
some of my favorite
people in the industry
—RACHEL DOOLEY

How happy I was
when I received my
CFDA membership
card in the mail!
—RACHEL ZOE

Being nominated
for the Perry Ellis
Award within a few
years of starting my
own business
—RAFE TOTENGCO

Being nominated, the
first time, and attending
the gala with James
Galanos at my side
—RALPH RUCCI

Attending my first
membership meeting
and realizing that every
name in the room is
also a label
—R. SCOTT FRENCH

Winning the Geoffrey
Beene Lifetime
Achievement Award,
giving my short
speech with Donna
and Calvin standing
next to me
—ROBERT LEE MORRIS

Receiving the call
from Lisa Smilor that
I had been accepted
into the CFDA
—SANG A IM-PROPP

When Alicia Keys sang "Happy Birthday" to me in my ear

—ITALO ZUCCHELLI

Meeting Princess Diana

—ROLAND NIVELAIS

Bringing in eleven palm trees, a rug, and mangoes for the fashion fund presentation

—WARIS AHLUWALIA

Receiving the CFDA
Geoffrey Beene Lifetime
Achievement Award by
Anna Wintour in 2012 was
an amazing honor and
one of the most memorable
moments of my career.

—TOMMY HILFIGER

The call from Robert Lee Morris, letting me know I had been accepted for membership

—ROD KEENAN

My first awards show last year.
To be sitting in the same room
with some of the people you
look up to and admire still blows
my mind away. It's like being
part of a special family.

—SHAUN KEARNEY

The smile on my mom's face when I told her I was accepted

—SIMON ALCANTARA

Hearing our names being
announced—and our wives
screaming—as we received
the Menswear Designer
of the Year Award in 2010.

—DAVID NEVILLE

The 100-year necklace. Each necklace has antique and vintage elements ranging from 1860 to 1960.

—LISA SALZER

A fluorescent red suit

—ITALO ZUCCHELLI

An Italian goat-suede sport coat. It is the ultimate everyday, unconstructed, travel sport coat.

—HENRY JACOBSON

Something for my sister when I was fifteen years old

—BIBHU MOHAPATRA

The woman's power suit

—ELIE TAHARI

A gown Joss Stone wore

—NICOLE MILLER

Sandra Bullock's silver dress she wore when she won her Oscar

—KEREN CRAIG

My headmistress dress

—L'WREN SCOTT

MY FAVORITE ITEM I'VE EVER DESIGNED IS

A rosary with clear-and-white beads—Celtic inspired—I wear it every day! And a San Benito ring that I have been wearing for more than ten years.

—CHERYL FINNEGAN

Levi's Apron Bag

—BILLY REID

A floor-length, rare golden-sable coat

—DENNIS BASSO

A simple, great white cotton shirt

—EDDIE RODRIGUEZ

A hand-stitched leather mosaic circle apron dress over a crazy printed silk dress

—AMY CHAN

The opening ceremony clothes for the U.S. Olympic teams

—HENRY GRETHEL

My wedding dress

—LAUREN MOFFATT

A pale-gray, silk chiffon jumpsuit and diaphanous coat covered in chiffon flowers and Swarovski—crystals—worn by the great actress Jane Lapotaire when she accepted a Tony Award for Best Actress in a Play (*PIAF*)

—KENNETH BONAVITACOLA

The interiors of our homes—a collaboration with my husband, Jonathan
—TRINA TURK

A suit that I love, my mom loves, my friend's grandmother loves. Seeing one look that's beloved by women at such different points in their lives is endlessly inspiring to me.
—LISA MAYOCK

The Ena dress
—MARIA CORNEJO

A series of conversation ties inspired by Erté designs
—MICHEL KRAMER-METRAUX

Carolyn Bessette Kennedy's wedding dress
—NARCISO RODRIGUEZ

A long, black velvet dress inspired by John Singer Sargent's *Madame X* which became my most famous dress
—ROLAND NIVELAIS

A convertible cotton coat
—SHELLY STEFFEE

The first shirt I ever sewed, in eighth grade.
—STEFAN MILJANIC

my wedding dress
—TESS GIBERSON

The dress I designed for Julia Roberts to wear in *Ocean's Eleven*
—LIZ LANGE

A crocheted maxi-dress that Tyra Banks wore in my Anne Klein show. Very sexy.
—LOUIS DELL'OLIO

Le Fleur Couture corset
—MAGGIE NORRIS

The ivory bracelet worn by Nastassja Kinski in the photograph *Nastassja Kinski and the Serpent* by Richard Avedon
—PATRICIA VON MUSULIN

My tuxedo jumpsuit
—RACHEL ZOE

Michael Jackson's glasses for his "This Is It" tour
—SELIMA SALAUN

A black, cotton poplin ball gown
—DEREK LAM

A charcoal-gray, wool flannel duffle coat with a jacquard stripe around the hem. It's my go-to piece when I'm feeling I need a little pick-me-up.
—R. SCOTT FRENCH

The constant creative change that comes with each season

—ALEXA ADAMS

Working and collaborating with many different creative people, learning from their perspective, and creating something better than any one person could have done on their own

—ARAKS YERAMYAN

Collaborating. And being around my creative team.

—CHERYL FINNEGAN

Observing people all over the world enjoying our eyewear—without them knowing that I am the designer

—CHRISTIAN ROTH

The fact that it lets me express myself creatively

—EDWARD WILKERSON

Working with fabric mills, traveling the world, and hopefully giving pleasure to others

—HENRY GRETHEL

The gratification when an idea in my head gets materialized in a garment in something tangible. And I love seeing people in my clothes.

—GABRIELA PEREZUTTI

MY FAVORITE PART OF BEING A DESIGNER IS

Always having to change

—ADRIENNE LANDAU

The everyday feeling of starting something new

—CAROLE HOCHMAN

Looking at my clothing worn by women I love

—CATHERINE MALANDRINO

Getting back the samples

—DANIEL SILVER

Seeing someone wearing our clothes on the street

—COSTELLO TAGLIAPIETRA

Designing, creating, making, engineering, understanding the customer, and collaborating with my team

—DAVID YURMAN

Being able to use my creativity

—OLIVIER THEYSKENS

All the work that goes into the collection, the story, the mood. It is mostly for me and terrific.

—GABY BASORA

Getting to collaborate with so many different creative people

—GILLES MENDEL

When you see a sketch turned into a first sample

—FLORA GILL

Meeting creative people, having women relate to my pieces, hearing that it makes them feel more beautiful

—IRENE NEUWIRTH

Helping people realize their potential

—JOHN PATRICK

Essentially the freedom to create things that other people enjoy

—KEANAN DUFFTY

Seeing my vision come to life in three-dimensional form

—L'WREN SCOTT

That becoming "inspired" is part of my job. Who else gets to say that about what they do?

—LISA MAYOCK

You get to make people look and feel good about themselves

—MARIA CORNEJO

Presenting the final collection

—MICHEL KRAMER-METRAUX

Our profession is such a luxury—just to make people feel better about themselves, keep them protected, and part of the big world

—MONIKA TILLEY

freedom —EDDIE RODRIGUEZ

I love the complete design process, from start to finish, beginning with transforming the two-dimensional sketch into the three-dimensional, finished garment. I also enjoy styling and collaborating with art directors, photographers, and stylists for advertising and marketing campaigns.

—KEVIN CARRIGAN

Working with retailers and customers. I learn so much from them. Their feedback is truly invaluable.

—PAMELLA ROLAND

Seeing my stuff on random passing strangers—it's that feeling of your babies having a life beyond you

—MICHAEL BASTIAN

When the creative juices flow and the ideas come faster than I can sketch them

—LOUIS DELL'OLIO

Solving problems in the most elegant way

—MARY PING

Being able to make women feel great about how they look

—CHRISTIAN SIRIANO

Research, going to museums and calling it work

—REBECCA TAYLOR

The same reason I hate it. Fashion is ever-changing and never stops.

—SHANE BAUM

Being able to make an impact on people's lives by dressing them and making them feel good. Fashion is a very powerful tool and does create many emotions. I love being part of that journey.

—SHAUN KEARNEY

Creating a concept and making it 3-D

—SHELLY STEFFEE

Trying to understand how women's lives are changing, and trying to figure out what it is they need to feel comfortable and beautiful

—SOPHIE BUHAI

Draping

—STEPHEN BURROWS

Making women look and feel beautiful

—TADASHI SHOJI

Having an idea in the middle of the night, sketching it, and going back to sleep with a smile on my face

—ROBERT GELLER

Having the ability to make the clothing that I really want to wear

—TESS GIBERSON

Working with color, pattern, and textiles

—TRINA TURK

Seeing my designs that make people happy, beautiful, and confident come to life

—VANESSA NOEL

Making things happen

—DIANE VON FURSTENBERG

Creating beauty with craftsmen around the world. As Stendhal said, "Beauty is nothing other than the promise of happiness." We're all looking for happiness, aren't we?

—WARIS AHLUWALIA

Tom Ford

—ROBERT LEE MORRIS

Rudi Gernreich

—BETSY JOHNSON

Coco, of course!

—BIBHU MOHAPATRA

Catherine Malandrino
or Halston

—ELIE TAHARI

Leonardo da Vinci—because his thought process ran on so many different planes

—ERICA COURTNEY

Armani

—BARRY BRICKEN

IF I COULD COLLABORATE WITH ANY DESIGNER,

Madame Grès

—CATHERINE MALANDRINO

Alber Elbaz of Lanvin,
or the Olsen sisters

—CHERYL FINNEGAN

Giorgio di Sant' Angelo

—DIANE VON FURSTENBERG

Thomas Edison—
his creativity would spark mine

—JUDITH RIPKA

Saint Laurent— he defined classic style

—TOMMY HILFIGER

Claire McCardell

—AMY SMILOVIC

Norman Norell
—GILLES MENDEL

Giorgio Armani
—HENRY GRETHEL

My favorite jewelry designer is Suzanne Belperron. She was a great Parisian jeweler born in 1900. She was known for her bold use of stones. I love the fact that she was a strong, successful

Georgina!
—KEREN CRAIG

Adrian
—L'WREN SCOTT

Wharton Esherick
—LAUREN MOFFATT

Charles James
—LELA ROSE

Oscar de la Renta— worship him!
—LIZ LANGE

Cristobal Balenciaga, Maria Cornejo, or Isabel Toledo
—NARCISO RODRIGUEZ

Coco Chanel
—ERIN FETHERSTON

Madeleine Vionnet
—TADASHI SHOJI

Claire McCardell
—NATALIE CHANIN

Halston
—RACHEL DOOLEY

DEAD OR ALIVE, IT WOULD BE

woman during a time when women were not a big part of the workforce, private business owners, or designers. She was a strong, creative, independent thinker.
—KARA ROSS

Proenza Schouler
—IRENE NEUWIRTH

Armani
—ISAAC MANEVITZ

Christian Dior
—LOUIS DELL'OLIO

Madame Grès
—LUBOV AZRIA

For women's, Geoffrey Beene and for men's the late great (and in my opinion underappreciated) Perry Ellis
—MICHAEL BASTIAN

Madeleine Vionnet and Schiaparelli
—MAGGIE NORRIS

Sonia Delaunay. I love the bold use of colors in her artwork. Her prints are iconic, classic, and timeless. They are as relevant now as they were back in 1885.
—RAFE TOTENGCO

My music, my MacBook, my crystal board, my artist's paper . . . and an eraser
—CHERYL FINNEGAN

My glasses, canned soup, iPhone, Taiwanese oolong milk tea, and music that makes me want to dance
—ERICA COURTNEY

Organization, cleanliness, creativity, vision, and execution
—ROBERT RODRIQUEZ

Great people, good ideas, fab music, sharp scissors, and a working sewing machine
—KEANAN DUFFTY

Music, magic markers, paper, muslin, scissors
—YEOHLEE TENG

Japanese fine-point pens, Evernote, books on tape, an organized jeweler's bench, and lots of beautiful design books
—LISA JENKS

Colored pencils, lots of scrapbooks, my camera, art books, and a good team
—MONICA RICH KOSANN

MY TOP FIVE STUDIO ESSENTIALS ARE

My eyeglasses, sketchbook, my Pentel P205, .5mm mechanical pencil, a pincushion, and some dark chocolate
—GILLES MENDEL

Sharpie calligraphic markers, paper, scissors, scotch tape, and casting wax
—IPPOLITA ROSTAGNO

A dedicated assistant, an expert tailor, yards of matte jersey, lots of black Prismacolor pencils, and a flesh-colored Magic Marker
—KENNETH BONAVITACOLA

WFUV 90.7, Juki straight stitch, my inspiration wall, my 1913 scissors, my pattern archives
—LAUREN MOFFATT

Pentel pens, stacks of blank paper, inspiration boards, black coffee, and my team
—REED KRAKOFF

English breakfast tea, bubbly water, trail mix with berries, seventies music, white flowers, big windows, and lots of sunlight
—RACHEL ZOE

Champagne,
flowers, balcony,
telephone,
and Brandon,
my assistant

—BETSEY JOHNSON

Pellegrino,
reggae, sunlight,
visitors, and
laughter

—GREG ARMAS

My great design
team, Red Bull,
protein bars,
coffee, and lots
of laughter

—DAVID MEISTER

My team, inspiration
boards, dried
California apricots,
raw almonds, and
a great playlist

—TORY BURCH

Books, lead pencil, tracing paper, fabrics, stencils, embroidery materials

—NATALIE CHANIN

White pinnable walls, black Sharpies, HB pencils, white map pins, and reams of white paper

—MICHAEL SMALDONE

Organization, music, incense, and uber creative, kindhearted people

—SIMON ALCANTARA

Raw unsalted almonds, Pandora, iced venti Red Eye, an endless supply of whiteboards and tacks, and Papermate Sharpwriter #2 pencils

—SCOTT STERNBERG

Watercolors, notebooks to fill with crazy ideas, Genmai chai tea, Pantone books, and collage boards

—STACEY BENDET

Constantly finding new
things I need to learn about

—BIBHU MOHAPATRA

That thirty years later,
I still love what I do

—DENNIS BASSO

Losing my namesake label.
And getting over it.

—DEVI KROELL

THE MOST SURPRISING PART OF MY CAREER HAS BEEN

That I never imagined myself being compared to the biggest
and most successful jewelry designers in the world

—ERICA COURTNEY

Having my logo on the
cover of American *Vogue*

—GEMMA KAHNG

Longevity. After thirty years I'm beginning to think
I'm starting to get the hang of it.

—GERARD YOSCA

That it's actually a career!

—JEFF HALMOS

Being in the CFDA
—JOHN PATRICK

Changing
professions from
architecture to
fashion
—LUIS FERNANDEZ

Learning that every failure
has actually been, in some form
or another, a success
—MELISSA JOY MANNING

That it even
exists at all—I
thought I'd be in
advertising or on
Wall Street
—MICHAEL BASTIAN

Launching Barton Perreira . . . for me
it was a dream come true!
—PATTY PERREIRA

Having my son in
the middle of it all
—RACHEL ZOE

That one piece
of jewelry has
turned into this
—JENNIFER FISHER

Becoming a women's designer
—SCOTT STERNBERG

Having my
own label
—ROBERT RODRIGUEZ

My success
—RALPH LAUREN

When the White House called
to buy state gifts for the different
administrations for the
First Lady to give as gifts
—STEPHEN DWECK

Balancing art
and commerce
—GREG ARMAS

That it has unfolded
exactly how I envisioned it
—ULRICH GRIMM

Build on my strengths.
Make sure I grow
exponentially from the
season before.
—ARAKS YERAMYAN

Do it right the first time.
—BARRY BRICKEN

Lost time is never found.
—BLAKE KUWAHARA

Collaborate. Matisse
said he "never avoided
the influence of others"
as inspiration and

If you don't believe it,
they won't either.
—SOPHIE BUHAI

Always trust
your point of view.
—HENRY JACOBSON

"Begin Anywhere"
—John Cage
—JEN KAO

You can look back,
but don't stare.
—JUDITH RIPKA

Always use great
fabric and never
sign off on something
you dislike.
—MARY ANN RESTIVO

There is always
something to learn.
—MICHAEL SMALDONE

Give it everything.
Push yourself and
inspire everyone
else around you
to do the same.
—MONICA BOTKIER

MY WORK MOTTO IS

a starting point for
exploring an idea.
Design and art are
collaborative processes.
—DAVID YURMAN

Do what you say.
—MARIA SNYDER

Be open to learning
new ways.
—EDDIE RODRIGUEZ

Design when
you're inspired.
—ERICA COURTNEY

Stay focused, be
fearless, and follow
your passion
and instinct.
—KARA ROSS

Stay open to
possibilities you
have never
explored before.
—KENNETH
BONAVITACOLA

Come strong, or
don't come at all.
—MARTIN COOPER

Carpe diem
—MONICA RICH KOSANN

The best is not
good enough.
—MONIKA TILLEY

If you love what
you do, it should
never feel like work.
Love what you do
and you'll never
have to work.
—PAMELLA ROLAND

Work hard and never lose your curiosity.

—TADASHI SHOJI

Find a way or make a way.

—FLORA GILL

Find something that you love to do and success
will come naturally. My dad told me this at a very
young age, and I will never forget these words.

—RACHEL ZOE

Success is not final, failure is not fatal. It is the courage to continue that counts.

—RAFE TOTENGCO

To be continued

—DONNA KARAN

Stay passionate and inspired.

—TOMMY HILFIGER

No rules

—VERA WANG

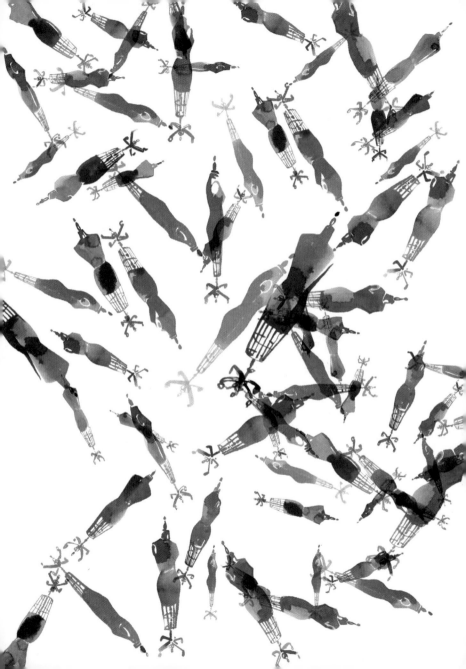

"Do everything."
Like Warhol said.

Rest on your
laurels

—CYNTHIA ROWLEY

Support others

Be jealous

—TORY BURCH

ALWAYS		NEVER
Create	ADRIENNE LANDAU	Stop
Take your time	BARRY BRICKEN	Rush
Half full	BETSEY JOHNSON	Half empty
Be kind	BIBHU MOHAPATRA	Be unkind
Follow your heart	BLAKE KUWAHARA	Say never
Be true to yourself	BRADLEY BAYOU	Give up
Believe	CAROLE HOCHMAN	Give up
No is not an answer	CATHERINE MALANDRINO	Give up
See any criticism as constructive	CHARLOTTE RONSON	Take it personally
Stay original	CHERYL FINNEGAN	Get greedy

ALWAYS | **NEVER**

ALWAYS		NEVER
Be curious, step outside the box	DAVID MEISTER	Take no for an answer
Give your opinion	DENNIS BASSO	Give up
Go for it	DIANE VON FURSTENBERG	Be scared
Listen to your gut	DOUGLAS HANNANT	Doubt an initial gut feeling
Enjoy every single day like it's your last	ERICA COURTNEY	Design when you're not inspired
Do it right the first time	GEMMA KAHNG	Cheat
Push your creative boundaries	GEORGINA CHAPMAN	Settle
Care	GERARD YOSCA	Say "good enough"

ALWAYS		NEVER
Love your work and be positive	HENRY GRETHEL	Be bored or compromise easily
Trust your point of view creatively	HENRY JACOBSON	Stop listening to those around you whose points of view you trust
Send a thank-you note	IRENE NEUWIRTH	Lose yourself in the success. Remember why you chose this job. To make gorgeous pieces that are passed down for generations.
Ask	JENNA LYONS	Assume

ALWAYS		NEVER
Keep your word	ISAAC MANEVITZ	Be afraid to try something that no one's thought of before
Say yes	JOHN PATRICK	Say no
Be prepared	JONATHAN MEIZLER	Make excuses
Love every minute	JOSIE NATORI	Stop
Believe in yourself	JUDITH RIPKA	Give up
Be empathetic	KENNETH BONAVITACOLA	Raise your voice at a coworker
Do what you love	KOI SUWANNAGATE	Not do your best
Persevere	L'WREN SCOTT	Give up

ALWAYS

Work hard

NEVER

Compromise

—JOSEPH ALTUZARRA

ALWAYS		NEVER
Try to start early (because it doesn't happen)	LAUREN MOFFATT	Wait till the last minute (because I do)
Seek inspiration	LOUIS DELL'OLIO	Stop learning
Evolve	MARCELLA LINDEBERG	Give up
When you stop learning, you stop falling	MELISSA JOY MANNING	Take no for an answer
Listen, learn, and move forward	MICHAEL SMALDONE	Regret
Smile	MICHAEL LEVA	Scream
Prepare	MICHEL KRAMER-METRAUX	Use shortcuts

ALWAYS		NEVER
Breathe	MIMI SO	Give up
Imagine it can be done	MONICA BOTKIER	Make a decision before thinking it through first. I had to learn the hard way since I am a very passionate, impulsive person usually.
Go for it	MONICA RICH KOSANN	Think it can't be done
Work	NANETTE LEPORE	Work late
Inspire	NICK GRAHAM	Conspire
Give your all	PAMELLA ROLAND	Settle or give up

Communicate

Doubt people's abilities

—LUBOV AZRIA

ALWAYS

Create a beautiful dream

NEVER

Create a delusion

—PRABAL GURUNG

ALWAYS		NEVER
Make it the best possible	PATRICIA VON MUSULIN	Let it out the door unfinished
Smile and arrive early	RACHEL ZOE	Appear entitled
Trust your intuition	RAFE TOTENGCO	Second-guess
Believe in yourself	RALPH LAUREN	Look over your shoulder
Push further	RALPH RUCCI	Just accept
Find a good partner who does what you can't do	REBECCA MINKOFF	Be snobby or act better than anyone, especially your fellow designers. We are family.

ALWAYS		NEVER
Try new things, stay forward	REBECCA TAYLOR	Live in the past, move on
Work hard	REED KRAKOFF	Give up
Make every piece carry your DNA	ROBERT LEE MORRIS	Copy
Have passion	ROBERT RODRIGUEZ	Lose it
Go with your gut	ROD KEENAN	Doubt your impulses
Work	SCOTT STERNBERG	Stop
Hope	SELIMA SALAUN	Give up
Be honest with your work	SHANE BAUM	Drink too much of your own Kool-Aid

ALWAYS		NEVER
Do your best and go with your intuition	SHAUN KEARNEY	Lose sight of your dreams
Solve and evolve	SHELLY STEFFEE	"Not try"
Do what you believe	SHIMON OVADIA	Give up if you've failed the first time
Be well mannered	SIMON ALCANTARA	Be rude
Do what you believe in	SOPHIE BUHAI	Design something you hate
Try your best	STACEY BENDET	Give up
Think positive	STAN HERMAN	Doubt yourself
Imagine	STEPHEN BURROWS	Give up
Stay true	TABITHA SIMMONS	Give up

ALWAYS **NEVER**

ALWAYS		NEVER
Keep an open mind	TRINA TURK	Say never
Believe in yourself	VANESSA NOEL	Give up
Put in the extra effort	ALEXANDRE BIRMAN	Give less than 100 percent
Prepare	MICHEL KRAMER-METRAUX	Use shortcuts
Create energy	JOHAN LINDEBERG	Look back
Try	LISA SALZER	Cry
Innovate	MARCUS WAINWRIGHT	Try too hard
Dream	VERA WANG	Give up

ALWAYS

Smile

NEVER

Hate

—STEVEN COX

PART 3

love

The not knowing

—GREG ARMAS

My partner (of thirty years), Eric Domege

—CHRISTIAN ROTH

To be in love

—BLAKE KUWAHARA

Geometry

—EDDIE BORGO

I LOVE

WE love: each other

—ROBERT TAGLIAPIETRA AND JEFFREY COSTELLO

My wife, my children, and my family more than anything

—TOMMY HILFIGER

Alan Siegel (my partner for twenty years),
Petey my Havanese (cutest dog in the world),
my family, and a great martini

—DAVID MEISTER

'nuff said

—SCOTT STERNBERG

My multiple and simultaneous careers. I love having had the opportunity to live, to work, to meet, to dress all over the globe.

—JOAN HELPERN

Sincerity

—DOUGLAS HANNANT

Unconditional love

—MIMI SO

The universe

—OLIVIER THEYSKENS

Dave

—SHELLY STEFFEE

Kind people

—SIMON ALCANTARA

Daniel

—STEVEN COX

Compromise
—BARRY BRICKEN

Loyalty and devotion
—JEFFREY BANKS

Happiness and to be
there for each other
—CHRISTIAN ROTH

Love is a state
of energy.
—SIMON ALCANTARA

A healthy obsession
—CHRISTIAN SIRIANO

Being comfortable in
your own skin
—PRABAL GURUNG

Honesty, loyalty,
and selflessness
—RACHEL ZOE

Absolute acceptance
and surrender
—CYNTHIA VINCENT

Wanting to be a
better person for
someone else
—GILLES MENDEL

You care about
someone and they
care about you
—NORMA KAMALI

Unconditional
acceptance
—JENNIFER FISHER

Everything
—KATE MULLEAVY

I'm still trying to
figure this one out.
—WARIS AHLUWALIA

LOVE MEANS

Putting those you
love ahead of
everything else
—HENRY JACOBSON

Life
—RON CHERESKIN

Acceptance
—MARIA CORNEJO

Colors of the rainbow
—MIMI SO

Mutual admiration
—ROD KEENAN

Continuous
admiration no matter
what time of day,
how you look or feel.
It's the smile and kiss
at the end of a long
day and a pair of
open arms.
—REBECCA MINKOFF

Being there through
thick and thin
—LISA SALZER

Putting yourself
second
—ISAAC MANEVITZ

Truly caring for
someone else more
than you care
for yourself
—MICHAEL BASTIAN

Giving
—SAL CESARANI

Accepting people
for who they are

—MELISSA JOY MANNING

Knowing someone
has your back

—DAVID MEISTER

Acceptance,
forgiveness,
laughter

—ERIN BEATTY

Me blush

—CHARLOTTE RONSON

Magic

—OLIVIER THEYSKENS

Life better

—CHRISTIAN ROTH

The world a better place

—DAVID MEISTER

LOVE MAKES

You glow

—GABY BASORA

The world a happier place

—ISAAC MANEVITZ

Err, lemonade?

—SCOTT STERNBERG

Me feel wonderful
every morning
and night, and helps
me get through
what happens
in between
—JAMES PURCELL

Everything else
fall into perspective.
It makes you
strong. It can also
make you weak.
—JENNA LYONS

You see the good side
of life
—ADRIANO GOLDSCHMIED

Everything else
seem ridiculous
—LOUIS DELL'OLIO

Me float!
—MARTIN COOPER

More love,
it's contagious!
—MONICA BOTKIER

Life beyond joyful—
illuminated
—RALPH RUCCI

You do things
for someone
you won't even
do for yourself
—R. SCOTT FRENCH

Me better
—SHELLY STEFFEE

All things possible
—STAN HERMAN

me crazy

—ERICA COURTNEY

A creative brain
dream outside the box
—JONATHAN MEIZLER

The world a hopeful
place to live in
—KENNETH BONAVITACOLA

Everything else
not important
—LAUREN MOFFATT

Everything worth it
—ALEXANDRE BIRMAN

You a whole person
—MONICA RICH KOSANN

Me creative
—PATRICIA VON MUSULIN

Babies
—PRABAL GURUNG

Everything in life
worthwhile
—RAFE TOTENGCO

All the bad in the
world go away
—STEPHEN DWECK

Me happy
—STEVEN COX

". . . you do wrong,
Make you come
home early, Make
you stay out all
night long . . ."
—Al Green
—WARIS AHLUWALIA

Said yes

—GREG ARMAS

Fill up a room with balloons

—CAROLE HOCHMAN

ROBERT: I carry a little heart
in my wallet every day that Jeffrey
hand-embroidered for me
our first year together.

JEFFREY: Robert still carries
the hand-embroidered heart I made
for him the first year we met.

—COSTELLO TAGLIAPIETRA

Ignore my weaknesses and celebrate my strengths

—TOMMY HILFIGER

Being by my side when darkness rules

—GABRIELA PEREZUTTI

THE MOST ROMANTIC THING

Putting love notes in my
luggage when I travel

—DENNIS BASSO

Love me unconditionally

—EDDIE RODRIGUEZ

Remember my birthday

—EDWARD WILKERSON

Say "yes"

—MARCUS WAINWRIGHT

Hide little watercolor
love notes in my luggage
when I was leaving town

—GERARD YOSCA

Nothing specific. To me, the small gestures are more meaningful than the grand.

—GILLES MENDEL

Letting me sleep

—LUBOV AZRIA

Buy me the bound copies of every issue of *Vogue* from the 1960s and 70s (my two favorite fashion decades) and my first job out of college was working at *Vogue*

—LIZ LANGE

To fly around the world to meet me for one afternoon

—PATRICIA VON MUSULIN

Send me love notes through a fax machine

—REBECCA TAYLOR

Baked potatoes in the kitchen New Year's Eve (with caviar!)

—ROD KEENAN

Not something I'd share in a book

—SCOTT STERNBERG

ANYONE HAS EVER DONE FOR ME IS

Getting a tattoo of my name one week after meeting me (he's my husband now)

—PAMELA LOVE

A few years ago my boyfriend flew into Paris for a night just in time to have dinner with me for my birthday. I was completely overwhelmed with happiness and love.

—RAFE TOTENGCO

Move across the country, and quit their job for me

—SOPHIE BUHAI

Walk the Alps and hold hands for the world to see

—STAN HERMAN

Being proposed to in a canoe in the middle of a lake

—TESS GIBERSON

Eat

—ARAKS YERAMYAN

Act like a fool

—BARRY BRICKEN

Am at peace

—EDDIE RODRIGUEZ

Gain a few pounds and see the world
through my sparkly rose-colored glasses

—ERICA COURTNEY

WHEN I'M IN LOVE, I USUALLY

Don't think of much else

—HENRY JACOBSON

Make the first move.
I chased my wife
for quite some time.

—ISAAC MANEVITZ

Eat too much, then say too much—in that order
—JENNA LYONS

Feel ten feet above the ground
—KOI SUWANNAGATE

Act like a fool
—LAUREN MOFFATT

Become oblivious to my responsibilities and daydream the time away. It's short-lived, luckily, because it's pretty bad for business.
—LISA MAYOCK

Am quite silly
—DEREK LAM

Am more creative
—VERA WANG

Tease, unmercifully
—LOUIS DELL'OLIO

Feel like I can bend light!
—MARTIN COOPER

Hum and dance
—MICHEL KRAMER-METRAUX

Feel inspired

—PATTY PERREIRA

Gain weight

—PETER SOM

Can't stop smiling

—RACHEL ZOE

Glow

—SIMON ALCANTARA

Feel like
I will live forever

—STEPHEN DWECK

Feel unusual things

—OLIVIER THEYSKENS

Am myself

—STEVEN COX

Wear orange

—NICK GRAHAM

Am ecstatic and can't focus

—TABITHA SIMMONS

My parents—
they were "mad for
each other."

—TORY BURCH

The moment I first saw
my son after giving birth to him. I
never fell in love so fast and so hard.

—ERICA COURTNEY

My mom

—GEMMA KAHNG

My mother

—WARIS AHLUWALIA

My parents, who are the most
amazing deaf couple and
have been together for over
fifty years—they are true
inspirations of love.

—KEVIN CARRIGAN

My parents

—DAVID MEISTER

I LEARNED WHAT IT MEANS TO LOVE FROM

The first time I laid my eyes on
my son. I have never felt so protective,
I have never thought of someone
else as being the most important thing
in my life. Now I think of him first.
I would do anything for him.

—JENNA LYONS

Being grateful
and giving love
to others

—LUBOV AZRIA

Learning
to love
myself

—SIMON ALCANTARA

Daniel

—STEVEN COX

My parents. They are truly the most selfless people I've ever known.

—LISA MAYOCK

My children. I've never known love so deeply until they were born.

—R. SCOTT FRENCH

Going to the Cayman Islands and getting engaged

—BARRY BRICKEN

The first one

—BIBHU MOHAPATRA

A day in the wine country—flying a glider, followed by lunch at Auberge du Soleil, and finishing up with a mud bath in Calistoga

—BLAKE KUWAHARA

A pick up at a bar on 53rd Street— that was it

—STAN HERMAN

When I met my wife at my cousin's wedding

—ISAAC MANEVITZ

secrets with and it was as natural as it could be. I felt so fortunate to be with this person in that moment. As goofy as it sounds, I knew then and there we would always be together. Now that's romantic!

—HENRY JACOBSON

A six-hour walk around Manhattan

—MARY PING

MY MOST MEMORABLE DATE WAS

July 1, 2004, the date my daughter was born

—CHERYL FINNEGAN

My first date with Ricky. We went to a pancake house in the Bronx and she recited Chaucer.

—RALPH LAUREN

Last night with my husband

—GABRIELA PEREZUTTI

Having lunch with my wife, Robin, on Union Street in San Francisco before we were married. I had just returned from a sourcing trip to Italy and was coming out of a previous marriage that had fallen apart badly. I was exhausted and in a terrible state, yet here was someone that I knew I could share my deepest

A blind date. I sat down with the wrong person for thirty minutes before realizing I was with the wrong guy.

—IRENE NEUWIRTH

The blind date I met my husband at Sapphire Lounge on the Lower East Side.

—REBECCA TAYLOR

Early in our relationship, Jac and I went to an outdoor bar in Oia . . . listened to Vivaldi, drank ouzo, and watched the sun go down. Very cool.

—LOUIS DELL'OLIO

My first date with Rodger twenty-two years ago

—RACHEL ZOE

The first date with my husband. It was lunch at Mad 61, which was the former restaurant in the basement of Barneys. We sat for hours.

—LIZ LANGE

Taking exotic trips with my husband to Belize, Mozambique, Cambodia

—MONICA BOTKIER

Sneaking into a public pool in the wee hours and swimming until dawn. Unfortunately this meant I was still wet when I went to my internship the next morning, but the staff politely pretended not to notice.

—LISA MAYOCK

the first one

—REEM ACRA

My joyous, endless first date with my husband

—SHELLY STEFFEE

In Paris at Hélène Darroze

—SIMON ALCANTARA

A picnic in my kitchen

—JEFF HALMOS

On a kayak in the Bayou and realizing that we were surrounded by crocodiles!

—SELIMA SALAUN

My second date with my wife, when I knew I had met "the one"

—R. SCOTT FRENCH

I would never kiss and tell.

—GILLES MENDEL

Wandering around Venice all day and then going for a late dinner at a small restaurant. It was a little hard to find but that was part of the fun.

—RAFE TOTENGCO

Loving yourself
—ALBERTUS SWANEPOEL

On TCM on the TV
—BETSEY JOHNSON

In a Bollywood flick
—BIBHU MOHAPATRA

The one you have with yourself
—ELIE TAHARI

Loving your life
—VERA WANG

I have a love letter that Orson Welles wrote to Rita Hayworth—it wasn't the longest relationship, but it was extremely passionate.
—CYNTHIA ROWLEY

Patti Smith and Robert Mapplethorpe
—JEN KAO

Scott and Zelda
—JOHN PATRICK

THE GREATEST ROMANCE OF ALL TIME IS

Romeo and Juliet, Clare and Leo–style
—LISA SALZER

My love story with my husband. It was a hard road that looked impossible and we beat the odds.
—GABRIELA PEREZUTTI

With yourself
—ITALO ZUCCHELLI

Impossible but perfect (Spencer Tracy and Katharine Hepburn or the Duke and Duchess of Windsor)

Elizabeth Taylor's love affair with jewelry

Are the ones that stand the test of time

—JUDITH RIPKA

Humphrey Bogart and
Claude Rains in *Casablanca,*
unrequited and brilliant

—KEANAN DUFFTY

One you can't
explain

—LAURIE LYNN STARK

Romeo and Juliette

—MARCELLA LINDEBERG

Cocteau's *Beauty and the Beast*

—MICHAEL SMALDONE

Tristan and Yseult

—OLIVIER THEYSKENS

One that
doesn't fade

—ROBERT RODRIQUEZ

A sense of humor and a
bit of unknown . . . too
much predictable is boring.

—CHERYL FINNEGAN

Passion, fantasy, and humor

—CATHERINE MALANDRINO

Being able to say sorry

—DANIEL SILVER

Truth

—DIANE VON FURSTENBERG

THE QUALITY I VALUE MOST IN A RELATIONSHIP IS

Patience

—ULRICH GRIMM

Passion

—DONNA KARAN

Trust and confidence

—FLORA GILL

Support and understanding

—GEMMA KAHNG

Acceptance

—GILLES MENDEL

Finding the same things funny

—KEANAN DUFFTY

Dependability
—DAO-YI CHOW

Humor and a "roll with the punches" attitude
—LELA ROSE

Being open-minded
—OLIVIER THEYSKENS

Mutual respect
—PATTY PERREIRA

Friendship
—RAFE TOTENGCO

humor
—NANETTE LEPORE

The ability to enjoy being with someone
without a single word having to be spoken
—R. SCOTT FRENCH

Authenticity
—SHELLY STEFFEE

Mutual respect and mutual inspiration
—SIMON ALCANTARA

Honesty, humor,
and ambition
—ZAC POSEN

Having a partner
in crime
—BLAKE KUWAHARA

Staying up all
night talking about
absolutely everything
—ERICA COURTNEY

Building a life together
—ERIN FETHERSTON

The sharing of
moments—good
or bad
—MICHAEL SMALDONE

The exposure to new
ideas, new ways of
looking at the world
and yourself
—JOAN HELPERN

Having someone
by my side
—ISAAC MANEVITZ

Never having to
make the bed
—JOHN PATRICK

Getting "the joke"
—LOUIS DELL'OLIO

Lazy Saturday
mornings in bed
—RACHEL DOOLEY

Having my best friend
so nearby all the time
—R. SCOTT FRENCH

The opportunity for
intellectual, emotional,
and physical intimacy
—HENRY JACOBSON

Knowing that someone
is always there for me
—ROBERT RODRIGUEZ

MY FAVORITE PART ABOUT BEING IN A RELATIONSHIP IS

Another opinion
—GREG ARMAS

It was natural for us
—SAL CESARANI

Having an ally and an
editor to share your
thoughts, adventures,
and questions openly
—FLORA GILL

When you can be
together, but silent
—GERARD YOSCA

Sharing and
creating ideas
—MARY PING

Trust and love. Knowing
there is someone who
ultimately has your
back, inspires you, and is
committed to building a
life together.
—MONICA BOTKIER

Sharing life's experiences
with the one I love
—PATTY PERREIRA

Learning about
someone else's interests
you would never have
found before. Having
a person open up new
worlds for you.
—SOPHIE BUHAI

Knowing that you'll
have a friend for life
—STEPHEN DWECK

Growing with
someone
—ZAC POSEN

Being in love!

—BETSEY JOHNSON

One plus one is not two—it's exponentially greater.

—DAVID YURMAN

Having doubled your troubles!

—SELIMA SALAUN

The chase

—MIMI SO

Don't sweat the small stuff

—PAMELLA ROLAND

Compromise!

—MARCUS WAINWRIGHT

Compromise and listening
(even if you don't want to)

—CHRISTIAN SIRIANO

THE SECRET TO A LONG-LASTING RELATIONSHIP IS

Always . . . forgiveness

—ULRICH GRIMM

I don't know yet, but I'm busy working on it right now.

—MAX OSTERWEIS

Not to believe forever is forever

—NORMA KAMALI

Passion, respect, and enough closet space

—BRIAN ATWOOD

Patience and being the first
one to say you're sorry
—ISAAC MANEVITZ

Having the same goals in life
—JOSIE NATORI

Friendship, laughter, and a good
bottle of Tignanello helps
—LOUIS DELL'OLIO

I've been married for forty-two years,
and I'm not sure what the secret is, but I do know
that you should never go to bed angry.
—DAVID YURMAN

The ability to see
greatness in your mate at a
time when they cannot
see greatness in themselves
—MARTIN COOPER

Overlooking
small annoyances
—MARY ANN RESTIVO

Compromise and commitment

—MICHEL KRAMER-METRAUX

Don't sweat the small stuff, learn to let things go

—MONICA RICH KOSANN

Mutual adoration

—RALPH RUCCI

Allowing each other to be individuals

—R. SCOTT FRENCH

Trust and communication. And love. You have to love each other no matter what.

—STACEY BENDET

A secret

—WARIS AHLUWALIA

Being creative and keeping it exciting

—GEMMA KAHNG

As Mark Twain said, "When you tell the truth, you never have to remember anything."

—NICK GRAHAM

ALWAYS		NEVER
Apologize	AMY SMILOVIC	Leave anything in writing
Pick your battles	BARRY BRICKEN	Say never
Be true	BETSEY JOHNSON	Cheat
Talk it out	BLAKE KUWAHARA	Go to bed without a kiss
Communicate	BRADLEY BAYOU	Take it for granted
Be committed	CAROLE HOCHMAN	Hurt
Stay free	CATHERINE MALANDRINO	Be possessed
Listen	CHARLOTTE RONSON	Lie
Keep something under your sleeve—something unexpected	CHERYL FINNEGAN	Go to bed mad
Listen	GEORGINA CHAPMAN	Comment

ALWAYS		NEVER
Trust, love, and keep your individuality	CHRISTIAN ROTH	Be dishonest
Be honest, laugh, and be supportive	DAVID MEISTER	Go to bed mad
Laugh	DENNIS BASSO	Go to bed angry—NEVER!
Treat that person like you did on your first date	ERICA COURTNEY	Be a jackass
Work hard	GABRIELA PEREZUTTI	Take for granted
Say you're sorry	GILLES MENDEL	Let the sun go down on an argument
Communicate in a healthy way	HENRY JACOBSON	Forget the importance of all forms of intimacy

ALWAYS

Have your own life

NEVER

Sweat the small stuff

—JENNIFER MEYER

ALWAYS		NEVER
Listen	IRENE NEUWIRTH	Be close-minded
Have fun	JOHN PATRICK	Be boring
Communicate	JONATHAN MEIZLER	Hold a grudge
Forgive	JUDITH RIPKA	Hold grudges
Breathe in and out	KEANAN DUFFTY	Just breathe out
Be truthful	KENNETH BONAVITACOLA	Lie
Give most of your French fries	KOI SUWANNAGATE	Make them give you any of theirs
Laugh	LAUREN MOFFATT	Get dramatic
Be selfless	LAURIE LYNN STARK	Overthink it—just be in it
Listen	LOUIS DELL'OLIO	Be cruel

ALWAYS   NEVER

ALWAYS		NEVER
Wait a day before breaking up	LUBOV AZRIA	Go to bed angry
Be true	MARCELLA LINDEBERG	Lose trust
Try	MICHAEL LEVA	Forget
Laugh	MICHAEL SMALDONE	Forget an anniversary
Stay the course	MICHEL KRAMER-METRAUX	Give up
Have great make-up sex	MIMI SO	Stop fighting with each other
Tell the truth	MONICA BOTKIER	Be afraid to share
Do	MONIKA TILLEY	Talk about it only
Embrace	NICK GRAHAM	Disgrace
Tolerate	PATRICIA VON MUSULIN	Berate

Listen to one another and compromise

Judge or try to change somebody; accept them for who they are

—SHAUN KEARNEY

ALWAYS		NEVER
Love	PRABAL GURUNG	Expect
Be kind	RACHEL ZOE	Hate
Kiss at the start and end of every day	RAFE TOTENGCO	Go to bed angry
Think first	RALPH RUCCI	React first
Acknowledge your partner	REBECCA MINKOFF	Make them wrong (not saying I am perfect)
Remember I am probably annoying sometimes too	REBECCA TAYLOR	Go to bed angry
Be honest	ROBERT RODRIGUEZ	Be dishonest
Respect	ROD KEENAN	Become entitled

ALWAYS		NEVER
Share	SANG A IM-PROPP	Share too much
Love	SELIMA SALAUN	Despise
Act with your heart	SHANE BAUM	Be mean-spirited
Have respect and intimacy	SHELLY STEFFEE	Say never
Be kind	SIMON ALCANTARA	Be mean
Love	STEPHEN BURROWS	Lie
Give	STEPHEN DWECK	Ask for anything; you'll get everything
Carve your own lane	DAO-YI CHOW	Do it alone
Communicate	JODIE SNYDER	Lie

ALWAYS

Treat the other person as royalty

NEVER

Assume anything

—ROBERT LEE MORRIS

PART 4

life

My accent

−ALBERTUS SWANEPOEL

My heritage

−BIBHU MOHAPATRA

You would have
to ask them

−GEORGINA CHAPMAN

THE FIRST THING PEOPLE NOTICE ABOUT ME IS

My voice

−DENNIS BASSO

My accent

−GABRIELA PEREZUTTI

My hairdo

−IPPOLITA ROSTAGNO

The gap in my
two front teeth

−IRENE NEUWIRTH

That I am 6' tall in flats, 6'3"–6'4"
in heels. Despite the fact that
it's been highly documented, people
are still surprised by my height.

—JENNA LYONS

How much I look like Cary Grant

—RALPH LAUREN

My accent

—REBECCA TAYLOR

My custom perfume

—SANG A IM-PROPP

I'm not sure I have the best
vantage point from which to answer
this question

—SCOTT STERNBERG

My very large pupils—that are
100 percent drug-free!

—SOPHIE BUHAI

My hair

—CHRISTIAN SIRIANO

Surrounded
by color

—ARAKS YERAMYAN

I'm in the sun

—BLAKE KUWAHARA

I'm
creating

—CATHERINE MALANDRINO

I feel pain

—MAXWELL OSBORNE

I am doing
something I'm
passionate about

—CAROLINA HERRERA

I'm testing my own limits

—MAX OSTERWEIS

I FEEL THE MOST ALIVE WHEN

I discover new things,
meet interesting people, travel,
enjoy art that interests me

—CHRISTIAN ROTH

I am telling
a story with a
good punch line

—CYNTHIA ROWLEY

I hike

—DIANE VON FURSTENBERG

I arrive in a new
destination

—DONNA KARAN

I am
wake-
boarding

—NICOLE MILLER

I'm taking a walk in fresh
air on a perfect sunny
day with a slight breeze
DOUGLAS HANNANT

I put my dress on a
woman and she loves it
—**GEMMA KAHNG**

I am walking on a
sandy beach
—**HENRY GRETHEL**

I'm doing the things
I love the most
—**HENRY JACOBSON**

I'm afraid
—**JEN KAO**

I'm in the ocean
—**JEFF HALMOS**

I am starting a new
collection
—**JOHN BARTLETT**

I'm biking in NYC
in the A.M. on my
way to the studio
—**JONATHAN MEIZLER**

I am around creative,
fun, adventurous, and
inspirational people
—**KEVIN CARRIGAN**

I'm making
something happen
—**LUIS FERNANDEZ**

I dance slowly to
Italian music
—**MICHEL KRAMER-METRAUX**

I am sharing my
collection and new
ideas with my clients
and team
—**MONICA RICH KOSANN**

I'm working on product
—**NICK GRAHAM**

I am designing
—**PATRICIA VON MUSULIN**

I'm breathing
—**RALPH LAUREN**

I find myself
living my dream
—**REEM ACRA**

I am meditating and a
flurry of brand-new ideas
come flooding into my
third eye, into my heart,
and then out through my
hands into manifestation
—**ROBERT LEE MORRIS**

I'm under pressure
—**TABITHA SIMMONS**

I am designing
and creating
—**VANESSA NOEL**

The command to lower
houselights comes over
the headset and the
models are all lined
up in first looks. That
moment of anticipation
is hard to describe, but
for sure, it's the ultimate
adrenaline rush and
affirms my choice
of careers.
—**R. SCOTT FRENCH**

I'm discovering some-
thing new, a cool
museum show, an
amazing flea market
full of crazy finds, a
conversation
with a newfound
interesting friend
—**SOPHIE BUHAI**

I'm driving down
the Pacific Coast
Highway (PCH)
—**TRINA TURK**

Riding the barrel
of a wave
—**YIGAL AZROUËL**

Losing memories

—CATHERINE MALANDRINO

Regret and public speaking

—CHARLOTTE RONSON

Boredom

—EDDIE RODRIGUEZ

Heights! I'm terrified of heights, but I try
to challenge myself all the time—I've zip-lined in Jordan
and even climbed down Mount Masada.

—ERICA COURTNEY

Failure

—CHRISTIAN SIRIANO

THE THING I'M MOST AFRAID OF IS

Losing my mind

—FRANCISCO COSTA

Not having
an opinion

—MARY PING

Being mediocre

—GABRIELA PEREZUTTI

Running out of time

—GABY BASORA

Being irrelevant

—MICHAEL LEVA

Failure

—GILLES MENDEL

Losing inspiration

—JOHN BARTLETT

Losing my senses or getting burnt by boiling water

—OLIVIER THEYSKENS

Not working

—PATRICIA VON MUSULIN

Boredom and mediocrity

—RACHEL DOOLEY

Snakes

—ROBERT RODRIGUEZ

Doubt

—ROD KEENAN

Boredom

—ULRICH GRIMM

Retirement

—ADRIANO GOLDSCHMIED

Indian street food

—BIBHU MOHAPATRA

Getting my laundry done by someone else

—BLAKE KUWAHARA

Irrationality

—OLIVIER THEYSKENS

Oysters and champagne

—CATHERINE MALANDRINO

MY GREATEST INDULGENCE IS

Bar Pitti

—CHARLOTTE RONSON

Living in sunny places close to the sea

—CHRISTIAN ROTH

Jelly donuts

—DANIEL SILVER

Chocolate! And massages!! (not necessarily in that order)

—DAVID MEISTER

Dark chocolate
—DONNA KARAN

Chocolate cupcakes
—ERICA COURTNEY

Unscheduled time
because that's how
you create the mental
space to become
inspired again
—ERIN FETHERSTON

Cheeses and wine
—GEORGINA CHAPMAN

Flowers
—MICHAEL LEVA

Quiet, thoughtful,
downtime for myself
to recharge my
energy and karma
—KEVIN CARRIGAN

Flowers—and the
time to garden
—LAURIE LYNN STARK

Prosciutto and
dark chocolate
—MARA HOFFMAN

French champagnes
—MELISSA JOY MANNING

Collecting art
and objects
—PATRICIA VON MUSULIN

Gemstones
—RACHEL DOOLEY

My friendships
—RAFE TOTENGCO

Ice cream
—ROBERT RODRIGUEZ

shoes

—GABRIELA PEREZUTTI

Dirty martinis
—GILLES MENDEL

Truffles and lobster
—JONATHAN MEIZLER

Time and silence
—JUDITH RIPKA

Shoes, shoes,
and more shoes
—KEANAN DUFFTY

Buying cameras and
drinking beer
—MARCUS WAINWRIGHT

Being alone for at
least two hours
—MARCELLA LINDEBERG

At this moment . . .
cinnamon ice cream
—MARTIN COOPER

Expensive perfume
—MARY ANN RESTIVO

Being all alone in
nature without
any other humans
or human sounds
—ROBERT LEE MORRIS

Free time
—ROD KEENAN

Eating Korean food
—SANG A IM-PROPP

Frequent massages.
Bushels of diamonds.
Bricks of gold.

—SCOTT STERNBERG

Margaritas

—STACEY BENDET

Daydreaming of the things that could have been, or still could be

—STEFAN MILJANIC

Whipped cream

—STEPHEN BURROWS

Iconic American art; I'm always looking for new
pieces to add to my collection.

—TOMMY HILFIGER

Sleep and chocolate

—TESS GIBERSON

Instagram. I love being creative with it
and connecting with followers.
It's a social media popularity contest!

—BRIAN ATWOOD

Sugar

—CAROLE HOCHMAN

Love

—CATHERINE MALANDRINO

My sketchbook. I only use Moleskine pocket-size
and a Pilot Razor Point pen.

—DAVID YURMAN

I CAN'T GET THROUGH THE DAY WITHOUT

A good cup of tea

—DEBORAH LLOYD

A few landline phone calls

—DENNIS BASSO

Dark chocolate and espresso

—GILLES MENDEL

Kale and dog kisses

—JOHN BARTLETT

Two espressos and some type of berries

—JONATHAN MEIZLER

Hot ginger tea— I never get sick

—MARTIN COOPER

A few daydreams

—NANETTE LEPORE

Twizzlers and coffee, not together; talking to my wife

—REED KRAKOFF

A scotch

—STAN HERMAN

A piece of good Italian French bread

—STEFAN MILJANIC

Coffee

—TESS GIBERSON

What I can put on that makes me happy!

—BETSEY JOHNSON

Love

—CATHERINE MALANDRINO

My mood

—CHERYL FINNEGAN

How can this day be better than yesterday?

—MICHAEL SMALDONE

I GET DRESSED THINKING ABOUT

How many hours until I can take these Spanks off?

—ERICA COURTNEY

What Rush Limbaugh is wearing that day, and hope we don't wear the same thing

—NICK GRAHAM

The promise of the day and night

—PRABAL GURUNG

Getting to work on time

—REBECCA TAYLOR

What story I want to tell that day

—RACHEL ROY

How I feel that day

—SHELLY STEFFEE

How I feel and who I want to be that day

—SHIMON OVADIA

How do I achieve comfort and elegance at the same time?

—SOPHIE BUHAI

What socks match

—STAN HERMAN

The weather

—STEPHEN BURROWS

Being late

—TESS GIBERSON

What shoes I want to wear— they dictate what I am going to wear at that moment

—VANESSA NOEL

All the things I forgot to do yesterday

—SHAUN KEARNEY

Reflect on the day's experiences and appreciate what I have
—ARIEL OVADIA

Take two Advil PM and wish on a star
—BETSEY JOHNSON

Shower, stretch, and pray
—CHERYL FINNEGAN

Start tomorrow's "do" list
—CYNTHIA ROWLEY

Kiss my wife
—DAVID NEVILLE

THE LAST THING I DO BEFORE BED IS

Put on my potions and lotions
—ERICA COURTNEY

Read a history book
—ISAAC MANEVITZ

Say a gratitude prayer
—JOHN BARTLETT

Put All Good Goop on my face
—LAUREN MOFFATT

Watch Jimmy Fallon!
—TOMMY HILFIGER

Take my vitamins.
The vitamin B actually
gives you amazing
dreams and ideas . . . good
advice for designers.
—MICHAEL BASTIAN

Call Rush Limbaugh and ask him what he's wearing tomorrow
—NICK GRAHAM

A little social media
and a good night kiss
—RAFE TOTENGCO

Floss
—REBECCA MINKOFF

Decompress over Korean junk-talk-shows
—SANG A IM-PROPP

Say thank you
—SIMON ALCANTARA

Knock on wood for good luck.
It is an old pagan belief
that was passed
through my ancestors.
—STEFAN MILJANIC

Capri—with no tourists

—AMY SMILOVIC

A city, culture, good food, a market, a museum—
and a sandy beach is always nice.

—CHERYL FINNEGAN

One with privacy

—CAROLINA HERRERA

Northern Brazil

—FRANCISCO COSTA

MY IDEA OF THE PERFECT VACATION IS

Family, friends, boat, canal,
bread, cheese, and a
nice chilled bottle of rosé

—ROBERT GELLER

When everything
works out—weather, logistics, etc.

—BRADLEY BAYOU

Doing nothing in
a beautiful surrounding

—GEMMA KAHNG

Salt on my skin
from my last dip
into the sea

—DEVI KROELL

No Wi-Fi

—MARY PING

Croissants in
Paris with
my husband
and girls

—LAUREN MOFFATT

Two weeks in Kyoto

—ZAC POSEN

Sea, sand, and discovery

—JONATHAN MEIZLER

Being at home in Mustique
with no Internet or cell reception

⌐L'WREN SCOTT

To have no plans

—LAURIE LYNN STARK

Quiet time with my family, a garden shovel,
and a grill that is fired up. And
of course, the occasional cold beer (or three).
—NATALIE CHANIN

Anything that makes you grow in mind and spirit

—MONIKA TILLEY

⅓ lounging, ⅓ shopping, ⅓ cultural attractions
—TRINA TURK

My ideal vacation is always surfing in Costa Rica.

—YIGAL AZROUËL

Joan Didion, Henry Miller, Mark Twain, Jonathan Franzen, Harper Lee, J. D. Salinger

—CHARLOTTE RONSON

Amélie Nothomb, Oscar Wilde, Huysmans

—CATHERINE MALANDRINO

Salinger, Lewis, Steinbeck

—GREG ARMAS

THE WRITERS WHO INSPIRE ME MOST ARE

Gabriel García Márquez, Tagore, Virginia Woolf

—BIBHU MOHAPATRA

Proust, Nancy Mitford, and Guiseppe di Lampedusa

—DENNIS BASSO

Proust

—GILLES MENDEL

Latin American authors:
Jorge Luis Borges, Julio Cortázar, and
Gabriel García Márquez

—JONATHAN MEIZLER

The Beat Generation

—KEANAN DUFFTY

Ayn Rand and Hermann Hesse

—ROBERT GELLER

Tennessee Williams

—KENNETH BONAVITACOLA

Musicians

—LUBOV AZRIA

Samuel Beckett and Susan Sontag

—MARY PING

Hemingway, Gabriel García Márquez, Shel Silverstein

—MONICA BOTKIER

Henry Miller

—NICK GRAHAM

Classic Greek writers

—PATRICIA VON MUSULIN

Paul Bowles, F. Scott Fitzgerald, Truman Capote, and Khaled Hosseini

—RAFE TOTENGCO

T. S. Elliot, Truman Capote, Tennessee Williams, William Shakespeare

—RALPH RUCCI

Charles Bukowski

—SHANE BAUM

William Shakespeare and Agatha Christie

—SHAUN KEARNEY

Dead

—ARAKS YERAMYAN

President Lincoln

—BARRY BRICKEN

Glinda the Good Witch of the North

—BETSEY JOHNSON

All of the women out there that manage a career, children, and a husband

—CHERYL FINNEGAN

My mother

—L'WREN SCOTT

Mother Teresa

—MAGGIE NORRIS

My grandmother who survived WW2 in one coat worn as a dress for two years. Her zest for life and positivity stays with me always.

—MONICA BOTKIER

MY HERO/HEROINE IS

Marchesa Luisa Casati

—KEREN CRAIG

Neil Young

—PAMELA LOVE

My older brother who was killed in action serving as an Airborne Ranger

—HENRY GRETHEL

Eckhart Tolle

— KENNETH BONAVITACOLA

Hillary Clinton

—ROD KEENAN

John Adams

—LOUIS DELL'OLIO

Frank Sinatra

—RALPH LAUREN

Someone who saves a life

—SHELLY STEFFEE

Benjamin Franklin and Wonder Woman. Unlikely pair, I know.

—MARTIN COOPER

John Lennon/ Angela Davis

—JOHAN LINDEBERG

Marilyn Monroe

—BETSEY JOHNSON

Hubert Givenchy

—BIBHU MOHAPATRA

Andy Warhol

—BRADLEY BAYOU

Theodore Roosevelt. He was as well read as a man of his times could be, and his vision extended well beyond his times. I would love to

Coco Chanel

—CATHERINE MALANDRINO
—CHARLOTTE RONSON

get his take on life in 2013 after he had a couple of months to get up to speed.

—HENRY JACOBSON

Queen Elizabeth

—CHERYL FINNEGAN

Bill Clinton

—KENNETH BONAVITACOLA

Mrs. Obama
—KOI SUWANNAGATE

Leonardo da Vinci
—DIANE VON FURSTENBERG

Steve Jobs
—ERICA COURTNEY

Oprah. And maybe we could drink a few Moscow Mules and hang out for a while too?
—PETER SOM

My father
—REED KRAKOFF

FOR ADVICE, IT WOULD BE

Michelangelo
—LUIS FERNANDEZ

Cleopatra
—MONICA BOTKIER

My father
—L'WREN SCOTT

FDR
—MELISSA JOY MANNING

My grandmother, and I'd ask her for her tomato gravy recipe
—BILLY REID

Oscar Wilde
—SHANE BAUM

To be a better
businessperson

—ALBERTUS SWANEPOEL

To have coffee
ready-made

—BETSEY JOHNSON

To fly

—BRADLEY BAYOU

To read minds

—CHARLOTTE RONSON

To see the future

—CHERYL FINNEGAN

To see what the next
day will bring

—ELIE TAHARI

To command
world peace

—IPPOLITA ROSTAGNO

To dunk a basketball
like LeBron James

—JEFF HALMOS

To speak Italian

—JILL STUART

To stop time

—KEREN CRAIG

To have a sense of
direction—and I don't
mean big-picture life
direction, I mean
simple geographic
direction. Is that too
much to ask?

—MICHAEL BASTIAN

To answer an
unexpected question
with a quick,
appropriate answer

—MICHEL KRAMER-
METRAUX

IF I COULD WAKE UP TOMORROW HAVING GAINED

To be scientific

—DENNIS BASSO

Singing

—DIANE VON FURSTENBERG

To be at peace,
always

—EDDIE RODRIGUEZ

To be able to paint
like Velázquez

—EDWARD WILKERSON

To stop time

—LISA MAYOCK

To either plug into
the creative channel
at will, or have the
ability to speak any
language I want

—MARTIN COOPER

To save all the
children in the world
from hunger

—RACHEL ZOE

To be everywhere
at once

—NICK GRAHAM

This is more of a
dream, but wouldn't
it be great if you
could be in two places
at once?

—PAMELLA ROLAND

The power to heal

—RAFE TOTENGCO

The ability to speak five languages fluently

—ROLAND NIVELAIS

To transport myself wherever I wanted whenever I wanted—without traffic

—ERIN BEATTY

Teleportation

—SCOTT STERNBERG

To speak and understand Chinese fluently

—TADASHI SHOJI

ANY ONE ABILITY, IT WOULD BE

To have an operatic voice

—KEANAN DUFFTY

To stop worrying.
I have neurotic tendencies.

—SOPHIE BUHAI

To dance like John Travolta

—KOI SUWANNAGATE

A good voice

—JODIE SNYDER

Wouldn't it be fun to fly?

—MICHELLE SMITH

Having amazing parents

—BLAKE KUWAHARA

Growing up in a country where
you have the opportunity to make
your life anything you want

—LISA MAYOCK

My team

—EDDIE BORGO

The cards in my deck

—GABY BASORA

My family, friends,
and the Altuzarra team

—JOSEPH ALTUZARRA

The good fortune of meeting great people

—MARY PING

I'M MOST GRATEFUL FOR

All of the experiences that have made my life what it is

—DAVID MEISTER

The amazing and inspiring
people in my life

—ERIN FETHERSTON

Friends and family

—STEVEN COX

The health of my friends
and family

—RACHEL ZOE

A long life filled with unending possibilities

—STAN HERMAN

The fact that I am able
to do this with my life

—RALPH RUCCI

The chance
I've been given
to make this world
a better place.
I hope I don't
screw it up.

—WARIS AHLUWALIA

A life filled
with creativity

—NORMA KAMALI

Traveling across Europe
with my grandmother. She
exposed me to art and fashion
at a young age and with
a spirit of adventure.

—ALEXA ADAMS

The day I arrived
in America

—BIBHU MOHAPATRA

MY MOST TREASURED MEMORY IS

Walking on the Great Wall

—CAROLE HOCHMAN

My father and how
he truly cared for the people
in his life

—CHERYL FINNEGAN

The moment I saw the birth
of my daughter, Isabel

—EDDIE RODRIGUEZ

Being bought by Henri Bendel on the day I was going to give up and throw in the towel

—JAMES PURCELL

My first show, which was held at the New York
Public Library in Astor Hall ca. 1983.
It was a magical moment; you could feel it
in the air and the reviewers agreed.

—MARY ANN RESTIVO

Watching my mom get ready for a night out

—NANETTE LEPORE

Playing on the beach with my
cousins when we were kids,
without a care in the world

—RAFE TOTENGCO

Collective memory of my ancestors

—STEFAN MILJANIC

Versailles 1973 event or 1973 (the year)

—STEPHEN BURROWS

Being with my mum

—STEVEN COX

Trust and
generosity

—CHRISTIAN ROTH

Being able to pick up
where we left off no
matter how much time has
passed between visits

—R. SCOTT FRENCH

Long talks and
longer laughs

—JEFFREY COSTELLO

Laughter

—JEFF HALMOS

Laughter,
spontaneity,
intelligence,
creativity,
and honesty

—IRENE NEUWIRTH

THE QUALITY I VALUE MOST IN A FRIENDSHIP IS

The ability to be myself and
share my secrets with someone
else. This has been extremely
rare in my experience, but when
it's been there, what a gift!

—HENRY JACOBSON

Loyalty

—MARTIN COOPER

Sincerity

—MIMI SO

Perseverance

—LISA JENKS

Unconditional
love

—KENNETH BONAVITACOLA

A sense of humor
and a love of
the ridiculous

—MICHAEL BASTIAN

Effort. It takes
a lot to consistently
talk, listen, and
stay connected.

—FRANCISCO COSTA

A good listener

—JAMES PURCELL

The ability to
be your truest self
around them

—REEM ACRA

To have a
patient ear

—STEPHEN DWECK

Honesty,
straightforwardness,
and loyalty

—TABITHA SIMMONS

Sensible
honesty

—TADASHI SHOJI

Sincerity, loyalty,
and sense of humor

—DANIELLE SNYDER

It happens almost every day

—GABY BASORA

I was watching a funny movie with my kids

—GILLES MENDEL

My sister was driving a stick shift last summer in Corsica

—NANETTE LEPORE

Every time I watch Bea Arthur in *Golden Girls*

—ULRICH GRIMM

THE LAST TIME I LAUGHED UNTIL I CRIED WAS WHEN

Skyler makes me laugh all day, every day.

—RACHEL ZOE

I read a cartoon in the *New Yorker*

—REBECCA TAYLOR

I saw *Julius Caesar* by Handel at the Metropolitan Opera

—PATRICIA VON MUSULIN

My daughter was convincing me to buy her a pair of gold shoes. She put them on and started dancing around the shoe department. She looked at me and said, "Mommy, these shoes are amazing! They already know my moves."

—CHERYL FINNEGAN

Other people's creativity. I love art, I love people with strong opinions that come out through their work.

—AMY SMILOVIC

Good energy and optimism

—ARIEL OVADIA

Art

—GERARD YOSCA

The streets of NYC

—EDDIE RODRIGUEZ

Fairy tales, photography, the 1960s, and Paris

—ERIN FETHERSTON

I'M ALWAYS INSPIRED BY

People who do the right thing

—BARRY BRICKEN

Lanvin and Central Park

—BETSEY JOHNSON

Women

—JOSIE NATORI

People who work to help make the world a better place

—DAVID MEISTER

My partner, Keren Craig

—GEORGINA CHAPMAN

Walking unfamiliar streets and shopping stores worldwide

—HENRY GRETHEL

People who make it because they persevere despite the odds

—EDWARD WILKERSON

Hard work and determination. Successful women.

—IRENE NEUWIRTH

Yoga

—JOHN BARTLETT

A trip to the library

—LISA MAYOCK

Mothers

—PRABAL GURUNG

My trips to the Metropolitan Museum of Art

—PATRICIA VON MUSULIN

Anyone who exudes self-confidence

—YIGAL AZROUËL

New York City

—LELA ROSE

Nature, always . . . and a good bottle of Chianti

—LOUIS DELL'OLIO

Photography and fashion

—MONICA RICH KOSANN

The whistle-blowers

—ROBERT LEE MORRIS

Old movies, music, and fashion from the 1960s and 70s

—RACHEL ZOE

Eighteenth-century France and the 1940s

—ROLAND NIVELAIS

Interior design

—SHANE BAUM

Strolling in Manhattan

—SHIMON OVADIA

The amazing creativity and
energy of Manhattan

—TOMMY HILFIGER

Colors

—STACEY BENDET

Love and history, of course

—WARIS AHLUWALIA

The world
around us,
my travels to
new places

—ALEXANDRE BIRMAN

Talent

—VERA WANG

The streets
and travel

—GREG ARMAS

Cinema

—ULRICH GRIMM

Young people
who think

—RON CHERESKIN

Film, music, and theatre

—SAL CESARANI

People
who give up
their seats

—YEOHLEE TENG

Architecture

—JENNIFER FISHER

Stories of
those who have
realized their
dreams

—R. SCOTT FRENCH

New York City and
the juxtaposition
of the new and old,
gritty and polished.
The people and
culture of the city
are unlike anywhere
else in the world.

—KARA ROSS

Classical radio

—BETSEY JOHNSON

My mom

—DAVID MEISTER

Disco

—ELIE TAHARI

The echo of
my mother's voice
in my head

—ERICA COURTNEY

Reggae

—LUBOV AZRIA

The things little
kids say—no
one will give you
the pure truth
like they will.

—MICHAEL BASTIAN

This American Life

—RACHEL DOOLEY

I ALWAYS LISTEN TO

Bossa nova music from the 1960s
and jazz standards from the 1940s

—ERIN FETHERSTON

Opera

—VERA WANG

My business partner and
best friend, Wendy Martin

—HENRY GRETHEL

The news . . . I am a news junky—
and every Yankees game

—LOUIS DELL'OLIO

My gut instinct

—SHAUN KEARNEY

Classical music—
the human voice—nature's
phenomenon

—STAN HERMAN

Morning Edition
on NPR

—TRINA TURK

The universe

—WARIS AHLUWALIA

Criticism. It's good
to know what
people think, doesn't
mean you have
to act on it.

—BRIAN ATWOOD

Always get up
and do your best.
That's all there is.

—BETSEY JOHNSON

Always look forward
and never dwell on the past.

—HENRY GRETHEL

Buy it in
a fun color!

—GERARD YOSCA

Grace
under
pressure

—PRABAL GURUNG

Never say never.

—DEBORAH LLOYD

Always be polite. Never be negative.

—DENNIS BASSO

MY WORDS TO LIVE BY

Boring
thoughts
make
boring
people.

—CHARLOTTE RONSON

Live each day
as if it were
your last because
one day you'll
be right.

—BLAKE KUWAHARA

Always look forward.
Never say never.

—DEVI KROELL

Buy less but buy the best!

—JAMES PURCELL

Keep it simple, sexy, and honest.

—MICHAEL SMALDONE

I am stealing this from Barry Diller . . . "Next." It says it all.

—LOUIS DELL'OLIO

Every problem has a creative solution.

—DONNA KARAN

Whatever energy you put out there, that's the energy you're going to get back

—ELIE TAHARI

Life is in the details. (And there are so many damn details.)

—NATALIE CHANIN

"Go confidently in the direction of your dreams! Live the life you've always imagined." —Thoreau

—MONICA BOTKIER

Live lightly and dream big

—DANIELLE SNYDER

You regret most of the things you do not do.

—RACHEL DOOLEY

Shine bright.

—SIMON ALCANTARA

Greatness is in the details.

—R. SCOTT FRENCH

Make it happen.

—SANG A IM-PROPP

Don't worry too much. Sometimes you're ahead, sometimes you're behind. The race is long and in the end, it is only with yourself.

—SHANE BAUM

We are here for
a good time
not a long time.

—REBECCA TAYLOR

Don't do things that
don't feel like you

—NICOLE MILLER

If you don't ask,
the answer is no.

—NICK GRAHAM

Be awesome today.
And every day.

—STACEY BENDET

Do not waste your life living
someone else's choices.
Chart your own path.

—STEFAN MILJANIC

Tomorrow is another day.

—STEPHEN DWECK

That which matters
most must
never give way
to that which
matters least.

—WARIS AHLUWALIA

Live in the moment.

—ZAC POSEN

Dare to dream

—VERA WANG

Always be yourself,
no matter what
anyone tells you.

—CHRISTIAN SIRIANO

Keep on truckin'

—DEREK LAM

There's always
a solution

—JODIE SNYDER

Create
energy
and
inspire
people

—JOHAN LINDEBERG

Be compassionate.
Treat people
with kindness.

—TORY BURCH

Live your dream.

—ANNA SUI

Do or die

—YEOHLEE TENG

ALWAYS

Keep going

NEVER

Stop learning

—BRADLEY BAYOU

ALWAYS		NEVER
Tell the truth and stand for what is right	BARRY BRICKEN	Lie, cheat, or steal
Smile	BETSEY JOHNSON	Be around poison
Be kind	BIBHU MOHAPATRA	Be unkind
Love	BLAKE KUWAHARA	Hate
Be determined	CAROLE HOCHMAN	Give up
Discover	CATHERINE MALANDRINO	Get bored
Be willing to try something new	CHARLOTTE RONSON	Be afraid to make fun of yourself
Listen to your intuition	CHERYL FINNEGAN	Do something that doesn't feel right
Listen to yourself	COSTELLO TAGLIAPIETRA	Listen to yourself

ALWAYS   **NEVER**

ALWAYS		NEVER
Work hard	CYNTHIA ROWLEY	Take no for an answer
Push forward	DANIEL SILVER	Look back
Collaborate, explore, be flexible, and do it with kindness	DAVID YURMAN	Lose the passion or lose sight of the horizon
Believe	DIANE VON FURSTENBERG	Doubt
Hang out with the most inspiring people you know	ERICA COURTNEY	Say never
La vie en rose!	ERIN FETHERSTON	Say, "That's impossible."
Be good to others	GILLES MENDEL	Be good at the expense of others

Before you diagnose yourself with depression or low self-esteem, first make sure you are not, in fact, surrounded by assholes.

Don't worry about being successful but work toward being significant and the success will naturally follow.

—RACHEL ROY

Be gracious	HENRY JACOBSON	Be intellectually dishonest
Own the space	JAMES PURCELL	Wear cheap shoes
Listen to your instincts	JILL STUART	Second-guess yourself
Look before you cross the street	JOHN PATRICK	Jaywalk
Respect	JONATHAN MEIZLER	Shut yourself off
Be positive	JOSIE NATORI	Regret
Believe in yourself	JUDITH RIPKA	Stop dreaming big
Meow	KEANAN DUFFTY	Hiss
Be empathetic	KENNETH BONAVITACOLA	Judge others

ALWAYS		**NEVER**
Do your best	KOI SUWANNAGATE	Regret
Persevere	L'WREN SCOTT	Be afraid to fail, it's still better than not trying
Look on the bright side of life	LAUREN MOFFATT	Take yourself too seriously
You need to shut out the negative noise and follow your dreams.	LIZ LANGE	Listen to the naysayers
Move forward	LOUIS DELL'OLIO	Deal from fear
Try your best	LUBOV AZRIA	Give up
Look for the light	MARA HOFFMAN	Linger in the dark
Love	MARCELLA LINDEBERG	Hate

Make people laugh

Speak foul (swallow, breathe . . . let it go)

—STEPHEN DWECK

ALWAYS		NEVER
Be appreciative	MARIA CORNEJO	Be rude
Try	MARY ANN RESTIVO	Is harder— we are all human
Try	MELISSA JOY MANNING	Doubt
Try	MICHAEL LEVA	Give up
Take a chance	MICHAEL SMALDONE	Stand still
Get up, take your saber, and charge!	MICHEL KRAMER-METRAUX	Stay in bed lazily
Try to find some peace	MIMI SO	Stop believing in yourself
Have fun	NANETTE LEPORE	Stop dancing
Move forward	NICK GRAHAM	Regret

ALWAYS		NEVER
Love life	OLIVIER THEYSKENS	Forget $E=MC^2$
Believe	PATTY PERREIRA	Say never
Follow your heart and do what you love	RACHEL DOOLEY	Be too afraid to try
Love	RACHEL ZOE	Be cruel
Believe the best is yet to come	RAFE TOTENGCO	Think the end is near
Do more	REBECCA MINKOFF	Accept weakness
Yes you can	REEM ACRA	Nothing is impossible.
Do unto others as you would have them do unto you.	ROBERT LEE MORRIS	Judge others or believe that we are separated from our Divine Creator

Be yourself	ROBERT RODRIGUEZ	Give up
Deliver on time, as promised, to friends as well as customers	ROD KEENAN	Burn bridges
Allow the universe to guide you in the right direction	SHAUN KEARNEY	Underestimate the power of transformation
Embrace	SHELLY STEFFEE	Oppress
Be optimistic in everything you do	SHIMON OVADIA	Take anything for granted— everything is a gift.

| ALWAYS | | NEVER |

Be loving	SIMON ALCANTARA	Be hateful
Be free in your being and in your thoughts. Be yourself.	STEFAN MILJANIC	Look back. It is already past!
Be happy	STEPHEN BURROWS	Worry too much
Reach for your dreams	VANESSA NOEL	Give up
Try to be nice	BILLY REID	Be disrespectful
Be grateful for what you have	ALEXANDRE BIRMAN	Waste time frowning
Lead by example	TOMMY HILFIGER	Forget to say thank you
Trust your gut	SHANE BAUM	Lose your integrity

Fight for what you believe in

Take no for an answer

—JODIE SNYDER

AMSALE ABERRA
REEM ACRA
ALEXA ADAMS
ADOLFO
BABI AHLUWALIA
SACHIN AHLUWALIA
WARIS AHLUWALIA
STEVEN ALAN
SIMON ALCANTARA
FRED ALLARD
LINDA ALLARD
JOSEPH ALTUZARRA
CAROLINA AMATO
RON ANDERSON
MIHO AOKI
GREG ARMAS
NAK ARMSTRONG

ERIN BEATTY
SUSAN BEISCHEL
STACEY BENDET
RICHARD BENGTSSON
CHRIS BENZ
MAGDA BERLINER
COOMI BHASIN
ALEXANDRE BIRMAN
ALEXIS BITTAR
KENNETH BONAVITACOLA
SULLY BONNELLY
EDDIE BORGO
MONICA BOTKIER
MARC BOUWER
BARRY BRICKEN
THOM BROWNE
DANA BUCHMAN

RON CHERESKIN
WENLAN CHIA
SUSIE CHO
DAVID CHU
EVA CHUN CHOW
DAO-YI CHOW
DOO-RI CHUNG
PATRICIA CLYNE
PETER COHEN
KENNETH COLE
LIZ COLLINS
MICHAEL COLOVOS
NICOLE COLOVOS
SEAN COMBS
RACHEL COMEY
MARTIN COOPER
ANNA CORINNA SELLINGER

COUNCIL OF FASHION DESIGNERS OF AMERICA MEMBERS

BRIAN ATWOOD
LISA AXELSON
LUBOV AZRIA
MAX AZRIA
YIGAL AZROUEL
MARK BADGLEY
MICHAEL BALL
JEFFREY BANKS
LEIGH BANTIVOGLIO
JHANE BARNES
JOHN BARTLETT
VICTORIA BARTLETT
GABY BASORA
DENNIS BASSO
MICHAEL BASTIAN
SHANE BAUM
BRADLEY BAYOU
VICKI BEAMON

ANDREW BUCKLER
SOPHIE BUHAI
TORY BURCH
STEPHEN BURROWS
ANTHONY CAMARGO
VINCE CAMUTO
KEVIN CARRIGAN
LILIANA CASABAL
EDMUNDO CASTILLO
JEAN-MICHEL CAZABAT
SALVATORE CESARANI
RICHARD CHAI
JULIE CHAIKEN
GREG CHAIT
AMY CHAN
NATALIE CHANIN
KIP CHAPELLE
GEORGINA CHAPMAN

MARIA CORNEJO
ESTEBAN CORTAZAR
FRANCISCO COSTA
VICTOR COSTA
JEFFREY COSTELLO
CHRISTIAN COTA
ERICA COURTNEY
STEVEN COX
KEREN CRAIG
PHILIP CRANGI
ANGELA CUMMINGS
EMILY CURRENT
CARLY CUSHNIE
SANDY DALAL
ROBERT DANES
MARK DAVIS
OSCAR DE LA RENTA
DONALD DEAL

LOUIS DELL'OLIO	JUSTIN GIUNTA	KEN KAUFMAN
PAMELA DENNIS	ADRIANO GOLDSCHMIED	JENNI KAYNE
LYN DEVON	GARY GRAHAM	SHAUN KEARNEY
KATHRYN DIANOS	NICHOLAS GRAHAM	ANTHONY KEEGAN
RACHEL DOOLEY	ROGAN GREGORY	ROD KEENAN
KEANAN DUFFTY	HENRY GRETHEL	PAT KERR
RANDOLPH DUKE	ULRICH GRIMM	NAEEM KHAN
STEPHEN DWECK	JOY GRYSON	BARRY KIESELSTEIN-CORD
MARC ECKO	GEORGE GUBLO	EUGENIA KIM
LIBBY EDELMAN	PRABAL GURUNG	ADAM KIMMEL
SAM EDELMAN	SCOTT HAHN	CALVIN KLEIN
MARK EISEN	JEFF HALMOS	MICHAEL KORS
MERITT ELLIOTT	DOUGLAS HANNANT	MONICA RICH KOSANN
LOLA EHRLICH	CATHY HARDWICK	FIONA KOTUR MARIN
KAREN ERICKSON	KAREN HARMAN	GRANT KRAJECKI
PATRIK ERVELL	DEAN HARRIS	REED KRAKOFF
GEORGE ESQUIVEL	JOHNSON HARTIG	MICHEL KRAMER-METRAUX
STEVE FABRIKANT	SYLVIA HEISEL	REGINA KRAVITZ
CARLOS FALCHI	JOAN HELPERN	DEVI KROELL
PINA FERLISI	STAN HERMAN	NIKKI KULE
LUIS FERNANDEZ	LAZARO HERNANDEZ	CHRISTOPHER KUNZ
ERIN FETHERSTON	CAROLINA HERRERA	NICHOLAS KUNZ
ANDREW FEZZA	TOMMY HILFIGER	BLAKE KUWAHARA
CHERYL FINNEGAN	CAROLE HOCHMAN	STEVEN LAGOS
EILEEN FISHER	MARA HOFFMAN	DEREK LAM
JENNIFER FISHER	SWAIM HUTSON	RICHARD LAMBERTSON
DANA FOLEY	SANG A IM-PROPP	ADRIENNE LANDAU
TOM FORD	ALEJANDRO INGELMO	LIZ LANGE
ISTVAN FRANCER	MARC JACOBS	RALPH LAUREN
ISAAC FRANCO	HENRY JACOBSON	EUNICE LEE
R. SCOTT FRENCH	ERIC JAVITS, JR.	LARRY LEIGHT
SHANE GABIER	LISA JENKS	NANETTE LEPORE
JAMES GALANOS	BETSEY JOHNSON	MICHAEL LEVA
JUDY GEIB	ALEXANDER JULIAN	NATALIE LEVY
NANCY GEIST	GEMMA KAHNG	MONIQUE LHUILLIER
ROBERT GELLER	NORMA KAMALI	ANDREA LIEBERMAN
GERI GERARD	DONNA KARAN	PHILLIP LIM
TESS GIBERSON	JEN KAO	JOHAN LINDEBERG
FLORA GILL	KASPER	MARCELLA LINDEBERG

ADAM LIPPES
DEBORAH LLOYD
ELIZABETH LOCKE
DANA LORENZ
NILI LOTAN
PAMELA LOVE
TINA LUTZ
JENNA LYONS
SARAH LYTVINENKO
VICTOR LYTVINENKO
BOB MACKIE
JEFF MAHSHIE
CATHERINE MALANDRINO
COLETTE MALOUF
ISAAC MANEVITZ
MELISSA JOY MANNING
ROBERT MARC
MARY JANE MARCASIANO
LANA MARKS
PAUL MARLOW
DEBORAH MARQUIT
JANA MATHESON
LISA MAYOCK
ANTHONY THOMAS MELILLO
JESSICA MCCLINTOCK
JACK MCCOLLOUGH
MARY MCFADDEN
KIMBERLY MCDONALD
MARK MCNAIRY
DAVID MEISTER
JONATHAN MEIZLER
ANDREAS MELBOSTAD
GILLES MENDEL
GENE MEYER
JENNIFER MEYER
B MICHAEL
CARLOS MIELE
STEFAN MILJANIC
DERRICK MILLER

NICOLE MILLER
MALIA MILLS
REBECCA MINKOFF
JAMES MISCHKA
RICHARD MISHAAN
YVAN MISPELAERE
ISAAC MIZRAHI
LAUREN MOFFATT
BIBHU MOHAPATRA
SEAN MONAHAN
JEFFREY MONTEIRO
CLAUDE MORAIS
PAUL MORELLI
ROBERT LEE MORRIS
MIRANDA MORRISON
REBECCA MOSES
KATE MULLEAVY
LAURA MULLEAVY
SANDRA MULLER
MATT MURPHY
BLAKE MYCOSKIE
GELA NASH-TAYLOR
JOSIE NATORI
LEANN NEALZ
CHARLOTTE NEUVILLE
IRENE NEUWIRTH
DAVID NEVILLE
ROZAE NICHOLS
ROLAND NIVELAIS
VANESSA NOEL
MAGGIE NORRIS
JUAN CARLOS OBANDO
KERRY O'BRIEN
MICHELLE OCHS
ASHLEY OLSEN
MARY-KATE OLSEN
SIGRID OLSEN
LUCA ORLANDI
MAXWELL OSBORNE

MAX OSTERWEIS
ARIEL OVADIA
SHIMON OVADIA
RICK OWENS
THAKOON PANICHGUL
MONICA PAOLINI
GREGORY PARKINSON
MARCIA PATMOS
JOHN PATRICK
EDWARD PAVLICK
MONIQUE PÉAN
GABRIELA PEREZUTTI
PATTY PERREIRA
LISA PERRY
JAMES PERSE
CHRISTOPHER PETERS
THUY PHAM
ROBIN PICCONE
MARY PING
JILL PLATNER
LINDA PLATT
TOM PLATT
ALEXANDRE PLOKHOV
LAURA PORETZKY
ZAC POSEN
JAMES PURCELL
JESSIE RANDALL
DAVID REES
TRACY REESE
WILLIAM REID
ROBIN RENZI
MARY ANN RESTIVO
JUDITH RIPKA
PATRICK ROBINSON
LOREE RODKIN
DAVID RODRIGUEZ
EDDIE RODRIGUEZ
NARCISO RODRIGUEZ
ROBERT RODRIGUEZ

JACKIE ROGERS

PAMELLA ROLAND

CHARLOTTE RONSON

LELA ROSE

KARA ROSS

IPPOLITA ROSTAGNO

CHRISTIAN ROTH

CYNTHIA ROWLEY

RACHEL ROY

SONJA RUBIN

RALPH RUCCI

KELLY RYAN

JAMIE SADOCK

SELIMA SALAUN

JUSTIN SALGUERO

LISA SALZER

ANGEL SANCHEZ

BEHNAZ SARAFPOUR

JANIS SAVITT

ARNOLD SCAASI

JORDAN SCHLANGER

LORRAINE SCHWARTZ

L'WREN SCOTT

RICKY SERBIN

RONALDUS SHAMASK

GEORGE SHARP

MARCIA SHERRILL

SAM SHIPLEY

TADASHI SHOJI

KARI SIGERSON

DANIEL SILBERMAN

DANIEL SILVER

HOWARD SILVER

TABITHA SIMMONS

MICHAEL SIMON

GEORGE SIMONTON

PAUL SINCLAIRE

CHRISTIAN SIRIANO

SOFIA SIZZI

PAMELA SKAIST-LEVY

MICHAEL SMALDONE

AMY SMILOVIC

MICHELLE SMITH

DANIELLE SNYDER

JODIE SNYDER

MARIA SNYDER

TODD SNYDER

MIMI SO

PETER SOM

KATE SPADE

GUNNAR SPAULDING

PETER SPELIOPOULOS

MICHAEL SPIRITO

SIMON SPURR

LAURIE STARK

RICHARD STARK

CYNTHIA STEFFE

SHELLY STEFFEE

SUE STEMP

SCOTT STERNBERG

ROBERT STOCK

STEVEN STOLMAN

JAY STRONGWATER

JILL STUART

ANNA SUI

KOI SUWANNAGATE

DAIKI SUZUKI

ALBERTUS SWANEPOEL

ELIE TAHARI

ROBERT TAGLIAPIETRA

VIVIENNE TAM

REBECCA TAYLOR

YEOHLEE TENG

SOPHIE THEALLET

OLIVIER THEYSKENS

GORDON THOMPSON III

MONIKA TILLEY

ZANG TOI

ISABEL TOLEDO

RAFE TOTENGCO

JOHN TRUEX

TRINA TURK

MISH TWORKOWSKI

PATRICIA UNDERWOOD

KAY UNGER

CARMEN MARC VALVO

NICHOLAS VARNEY

JOHN VARVATOS

CYNTHIA VINCENT

ADRIENNE VITTADINI

DIANE VON FURSTENBERG

PATRICIA VON MUSULIN

MARCUS WAINWRIGHT

TOM WALKO

ALEXANDER WANG

VERA WANG

CATHY WATERMAN

HEIDI WEISEL

STUART WEITZMAN

TRISH WESCOAT POUND

CARLA WESTCOTT

JOHN WHITLEDGE

EDWARD WILKERSON

BRIAN WOLK

GARY WOLKOWITZ

JASON WU

ARAKS YERAMYAN

GERARD YOSCA

DAVID YURMAN

GABRIELLA ZANZANI

KATRIN ZIMMERMANN

RACHEL ZOE

ITALO ZUCCHELLI